Paule

TRICKY, BUT SOLVABLE!

Anne

CONTENT

© Wolfgang Kulla 2022
All rights reserved!
Herstellung und Verlag:
BoD – Books on Demand, Norderstedt
ISBN: 9783756203895

This riddle book
belongs

_____

Hello, ...

It's nice that you want to solve the riddles.

Our names are Anne and Paule. We go in the kindergarten. Soon we will go to school and we are looking forward to it. With this puzzle book there will be no boredom. You'll see that a wide variety of topics are addressed and you'll have to think about a lot of things. But that's what's so exciting, and it's sure to be a lot of fun.

Of course, you can't do it alone. Mom, Dad, Grandma, Grandpa, Aunt, Uncle or your big brothers and sisters will have to help you. They will read the texts to you and give you this or that hint. But you will find the solutions on your own.

We wish you much success!
Your Anne and your Paule

What's wrong here?

Some things are not right here! Do you see that too? What is wrong? What's true? Tell your mom / dad and tick "Yes" or "No" at!

Yes   No

Yes   No

6

Joke questions

Now it's getting puzzling! Questions about questions - can you answer it? You should not be sure, then look for the right one picture on the next page.
Here we go:

1. It hangs on the wall and shakes hands with everyone.

2. It hangs on the wall - without nails and screws.

3. What man can neither speak nor hear?

4. Who is born gray-haired?

5. Which images can you only see in the dark?

6. What rooster can never crow?

7. What has no feet, but when it's cold, it runs anyway?

8. Who hears everything but never says anything?

Here are the answers - select the correct picture and write the number of the question below it.

☐   ☐   ☐

☐   ☐   ☐

☐   ☐

paint and draw

That the funny guy is a bear, is easy to recognize.

Connect the black dots with a pencil and color the bear with colored pencils.

There are among others the brown bear, the black bear and the polar bear.

Which colors do you choose?

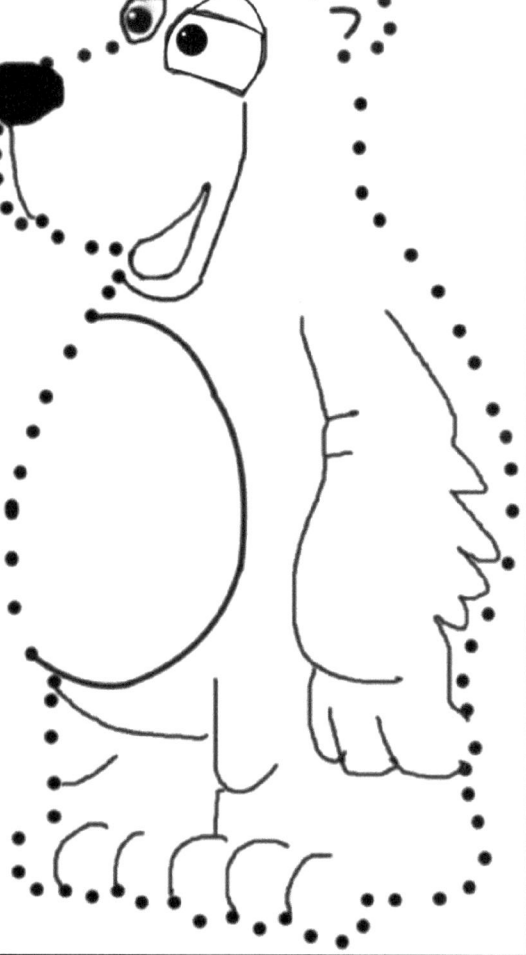

Do you feel like drawing a hen with chicks?
Connect the dots with a pencil,
then color with the crayons.

I want to draw a fish. Will you join me? Step by step I'll show you how to do it.
Take a sheet of paper and a pencil. Here we go:

1)

2)

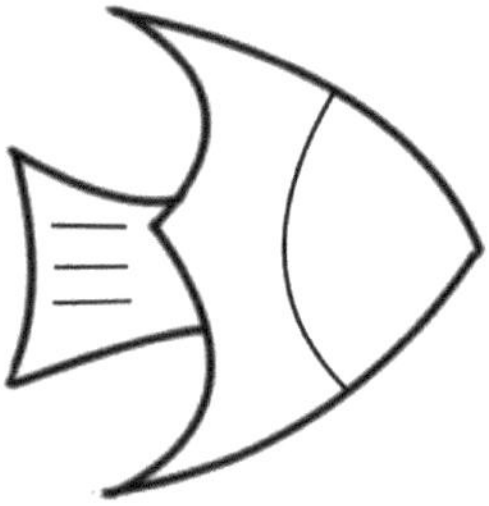

3)

4)

5)

6)

Color your fish with the crayons!

I prefer to paint a puppy.
Try it once! You will need a sheet
of paper, a pencil and crayons.
Here are the painting steps:

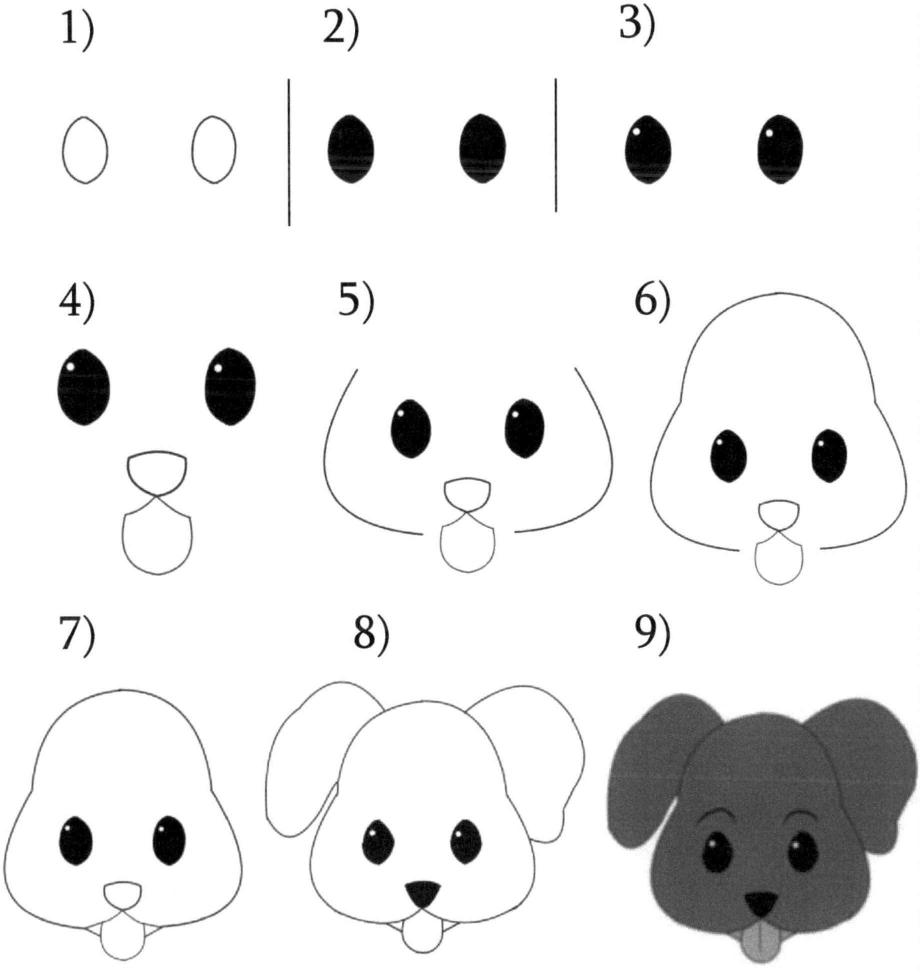

1)

2)

3)

4)

5)

6)

7)

8)

9)

How about a bear?
You will need a sheet of paper,
a pencil and crayons. Here are
the painting steps:

Color a mother cat with child!

Nature and environment

Insects are very important for nature. Many species are threatened with extinction. Find out what these insects like to eat most! Write the number in the respective circle!

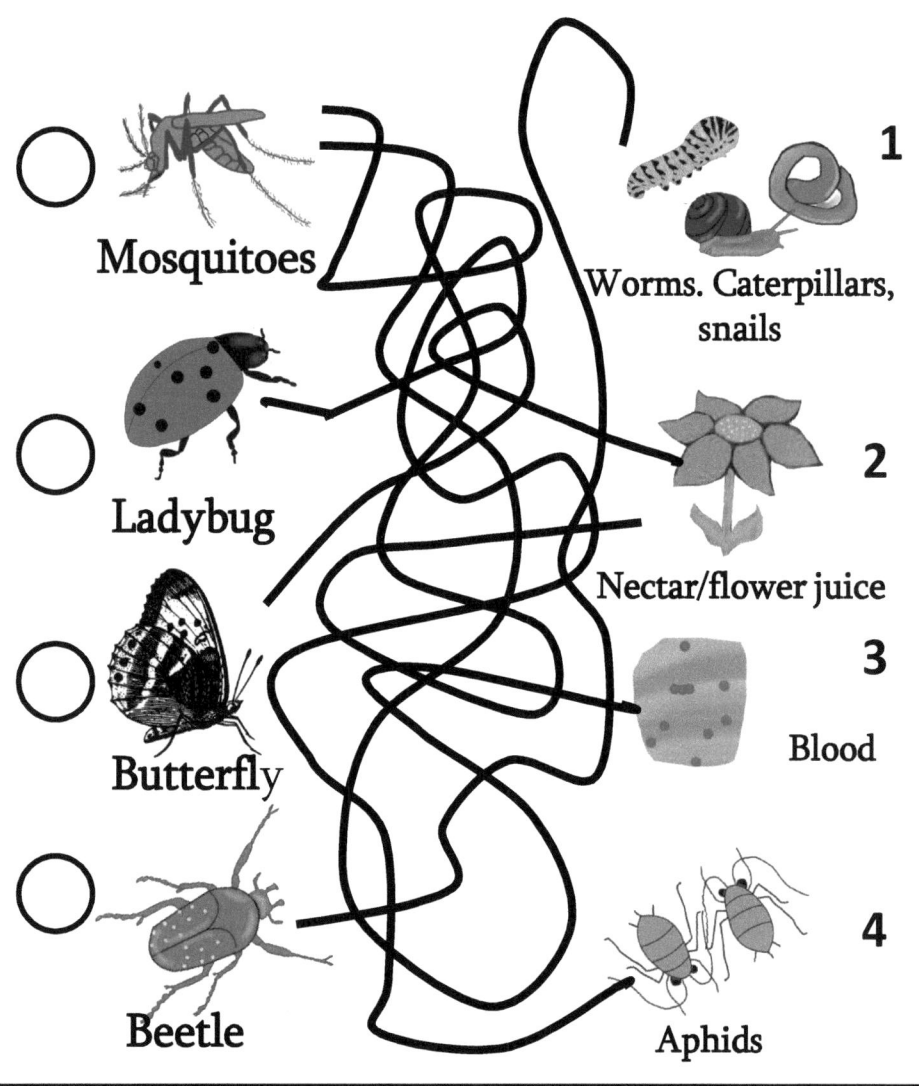

Mosquitoes

1 Worms. Caterpillars, snails

Ladybug

2 Nectar/flower juice

Butterfly

3 Blood

Beetle

4 Aphids

In order for everything to grow and thrive, nature needs bees above all. They feed from the sap of flowers. I think about how food and nesting sites can be created. What do you think? Tick the right!

Balcony flowers

The laying of large stones in the front garden.

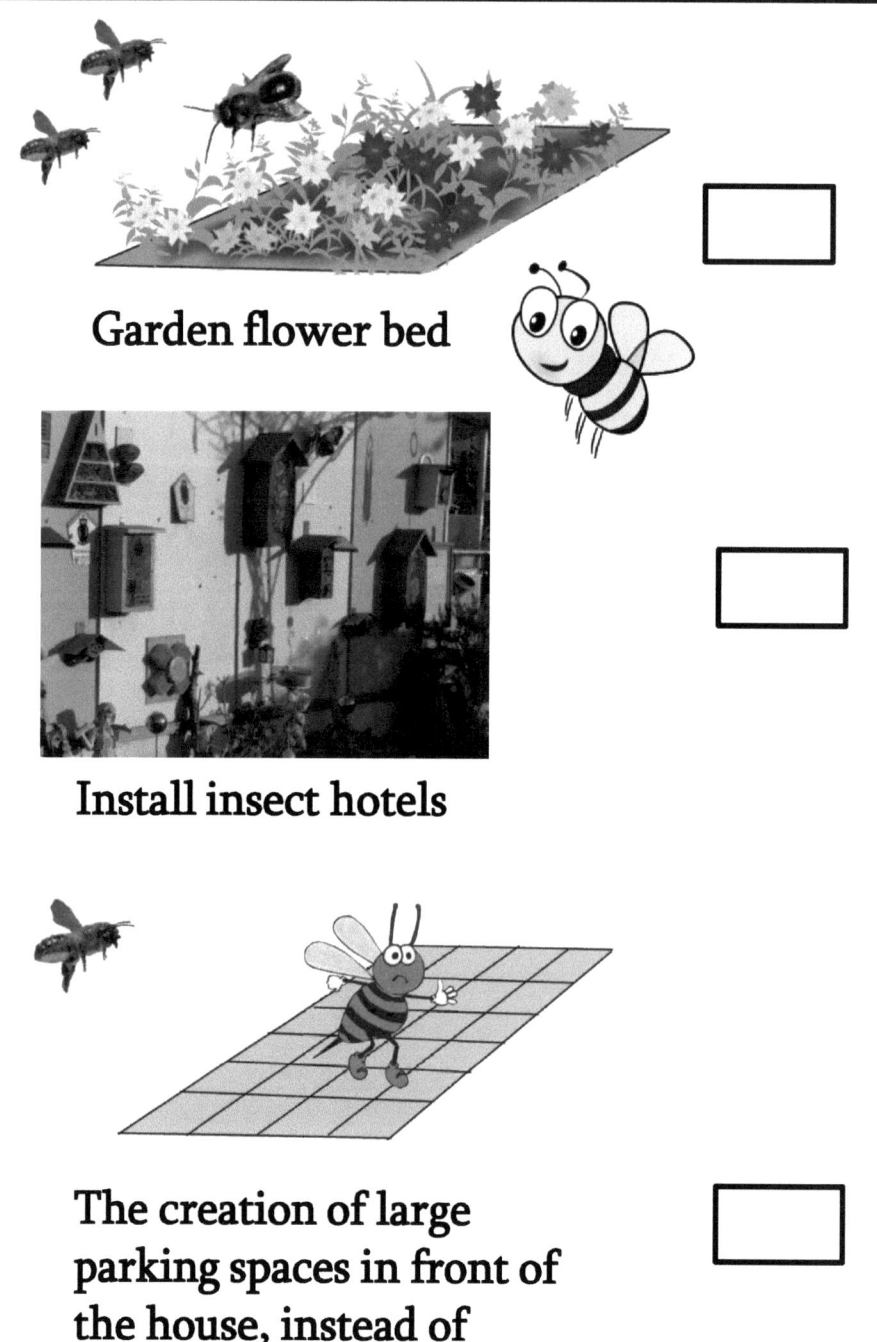

Garden flower bed

Install insect hotels

The creation of large parking spaces in front of the house, instead of flower beds.

Find out what the birds like to eat most! Write the number in the respective circle!

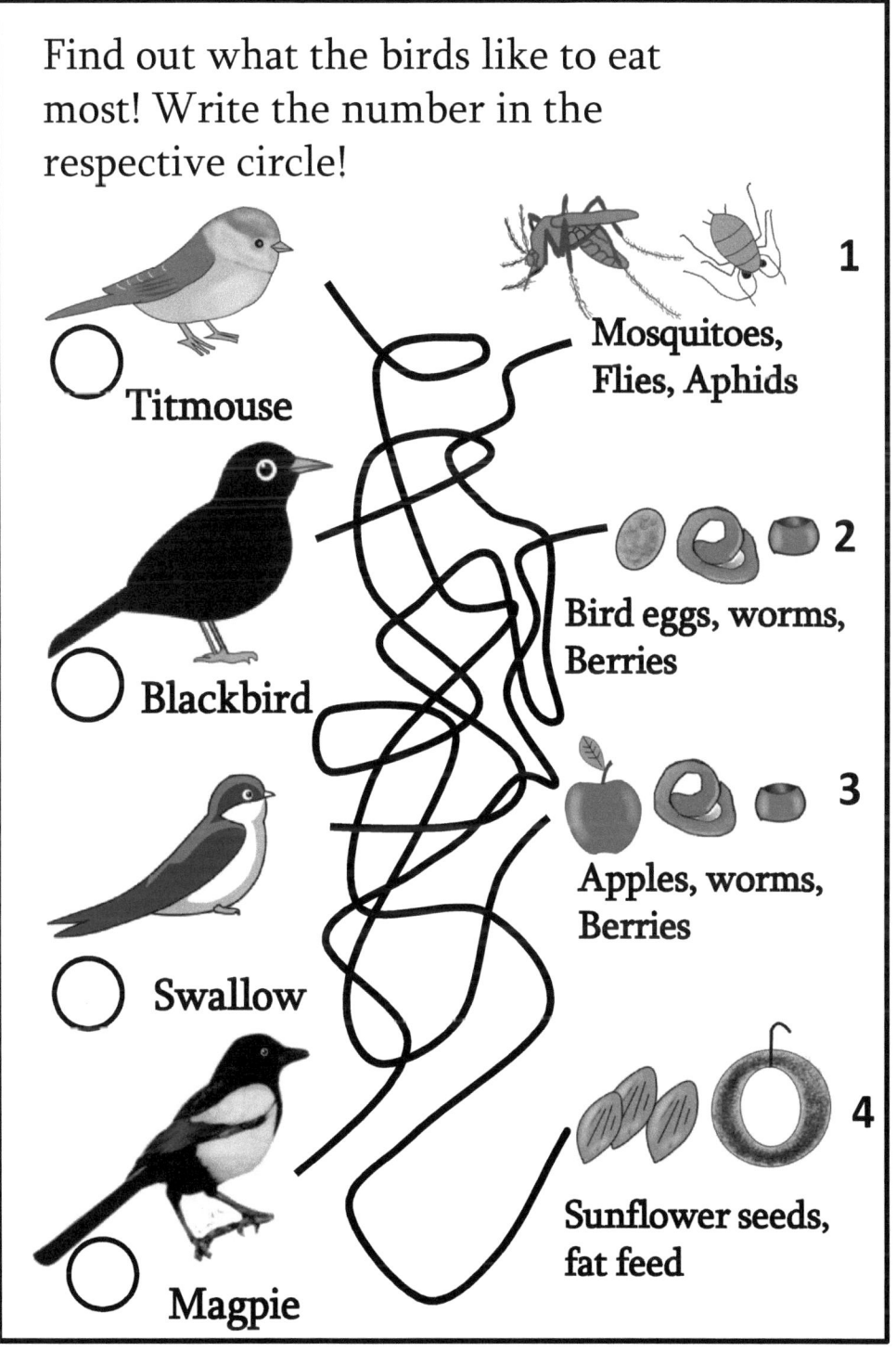

Titmouse

Blackbird

Swallow

Magpie

1 Mosquitoes, Flies, Aphids

2 Bird eggs, worms, Berries

3 Apples, worms, Berries

4 Sunflower seeds, fat feed

Our kindergarten groups want to collect the garbage on the meadow. What does not belong a meadow? Mark the corresponding points with a pencil!

Glass bottle ☐

Flowers ☐

Newspaper/ Paper ☐

Tin ☐

Face mask ☐

Grass ☐

Plastic cup ☐

Ants ☐

Paper handkerchiefs ☐

We are very concerned about the pollution of the oceans. Find out what does not belong in the sea. Circle the items with a crayon!

Fairy tale puzzles

What did the three little pigs build their houses out of?

From straw, from brushwood, from Bricks

In which fairy tale there is an bad luck - Marie?

Mrs. Holle

Who lives in the gingerbread house in which fairy tale?

Hansel and Gretel - the witch

What did Cinderella lose on the third day in the king's castle?

left shoe

"The Frog Prince" - What fell into the well of the princess?

one golden ball

What is the name of the boy
who climbs a beanstalk?

Jack

"The Wolf and the Seven
Young Goats"
Where is the seventh goat
hiding when the wolf enters
the house?

in the watch case

A miller had three sons.
When he died the eldest was
given the mill, the second the
donkey and the third got a
tomcat. What is the fairy tale called?

Puss in Boots

What does Little Red Riding Hood
do in the fairy tale "Little Red Riding
Hood and the Wolf" on the way
to the grandmother?

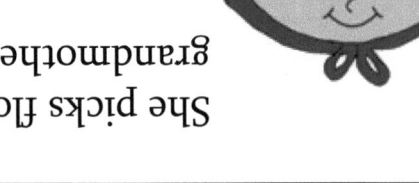

She picks flowers for the
grandmother.

"Anne...", my mum calls, "... go brush your teeth!"
I think about what I need to do this and how often during the day do I need to brush my teeth? Can you help me? Mark the corresponding boxes with a pencil!

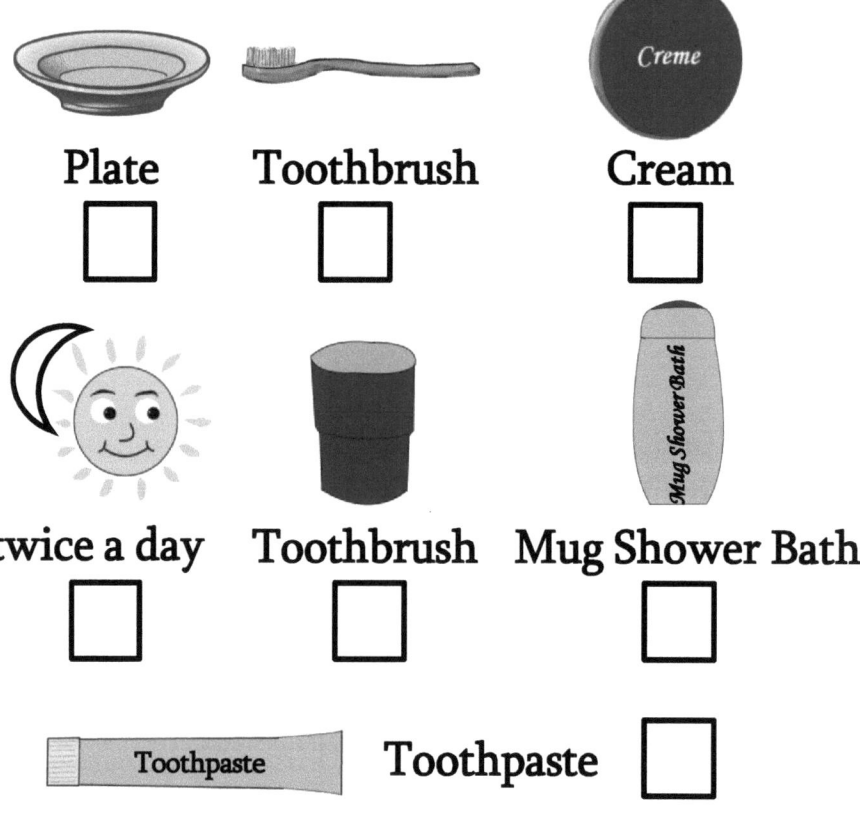

Plate ☐

Toothbrush ☐

Cream ☐

twice a day ☐

Toothbrush ☐

Mug Shower Bath ☐

Toothpaste ☐

I come from the playground and my hands are dirty. My dad immediately says:
"Paule, go wash your hands!"
What do I need to do that?
Can you help me?
Mark the corresponding boxes with a pencil!

Water

☐

Toilet paper

☐

Towel

☐

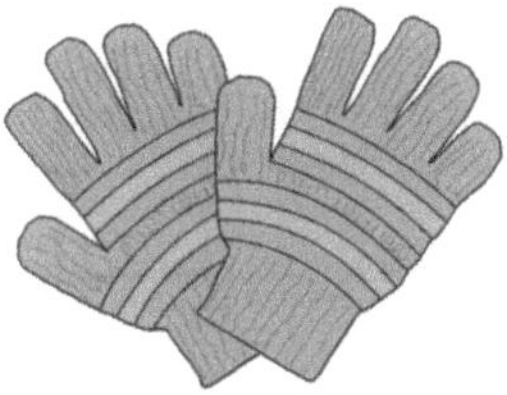

Gloves

☐

Soap

☐

**Time:
20-30 seconds**

☐

I ask myself: When should one absolutely wash the hands?
Do you have suggestions? Tick the boxes!

before the meal

after the toilet ☐

☐

after the evening greeting on television ☐

after feeding and Petting animals ☐

after the child comes home ☐

before playing on the playground ☐

Spatial vision

A wooden pin must be inserted in each hole. Which wooden peg fits into which hole? Write the the number in the box with a pencil.

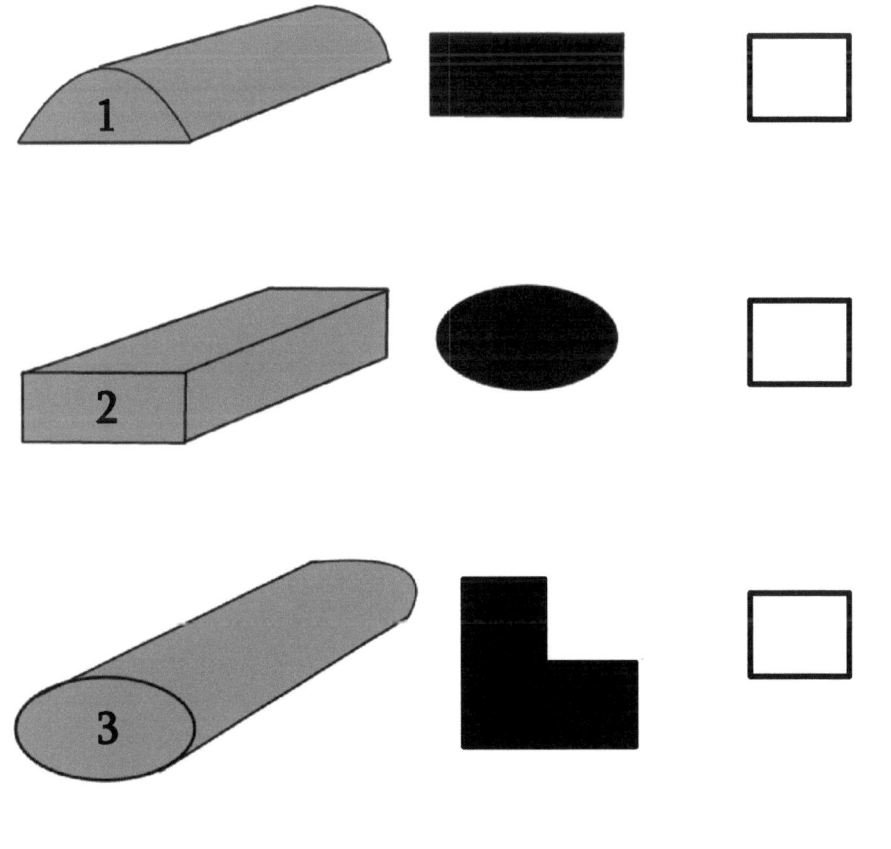

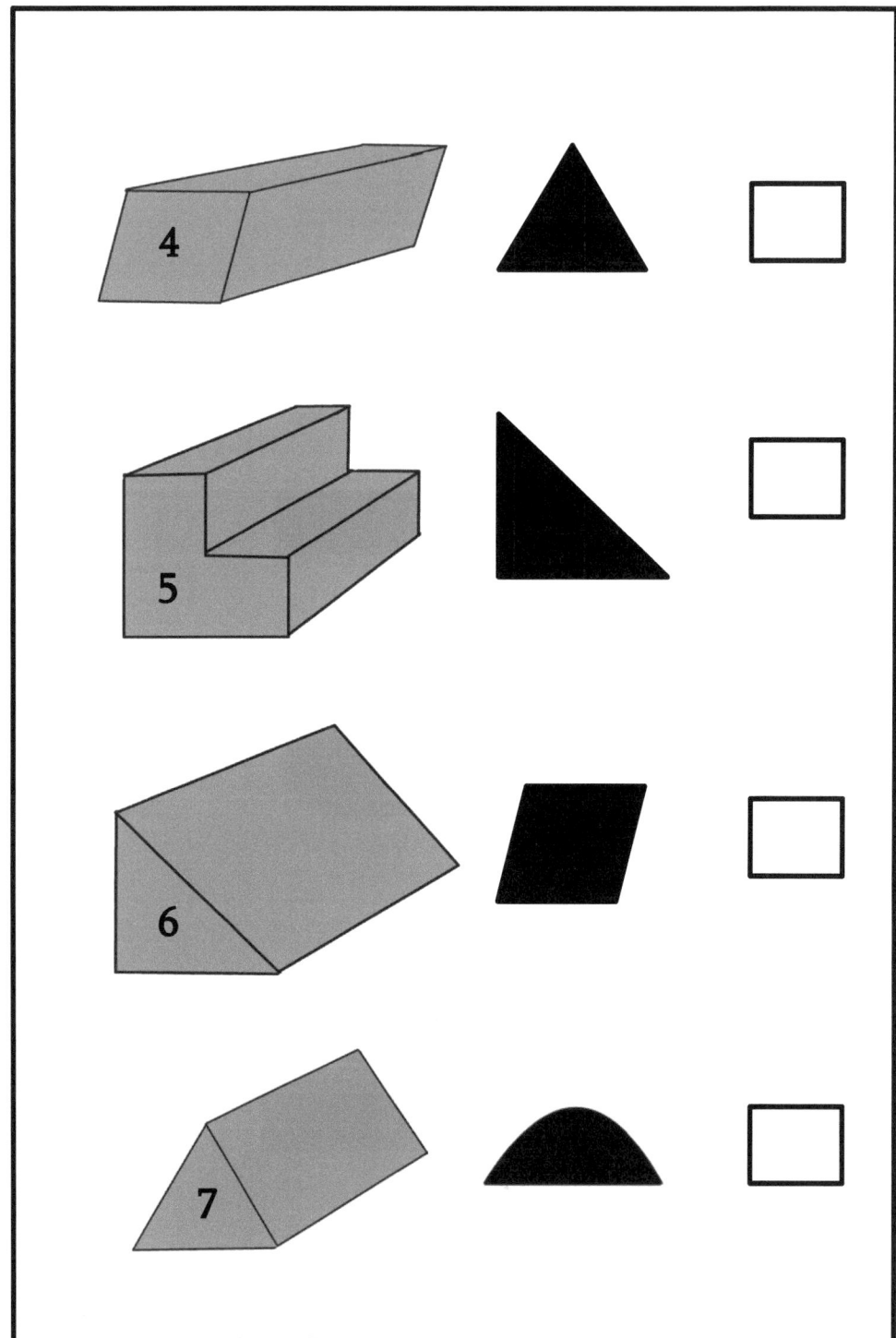

What does the last figure look like?
Draw the black square (dot) in the
last figure!

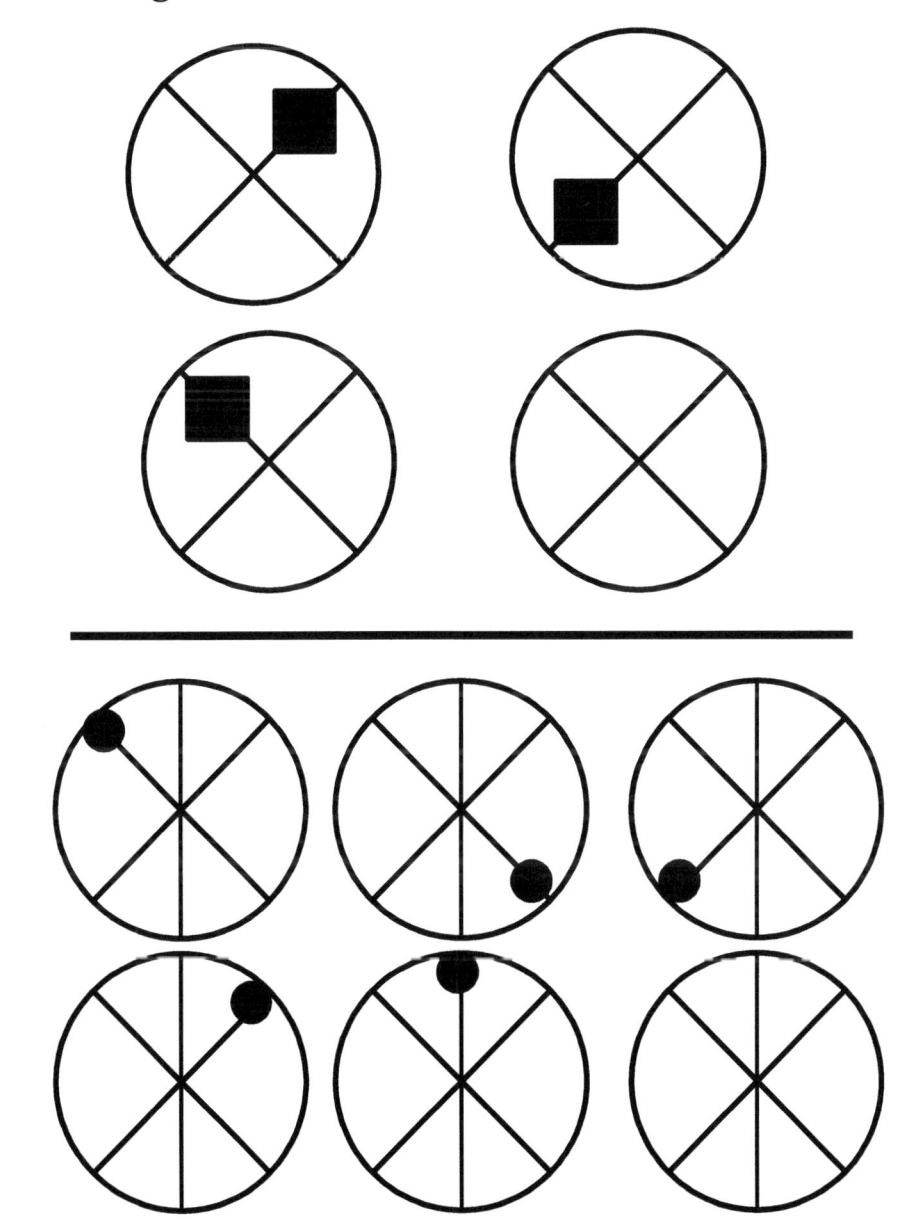

A puzzle on the left row can be put into
a puzzle on the right row.
Which puzzle pieces belong together?
Connect them with a line!

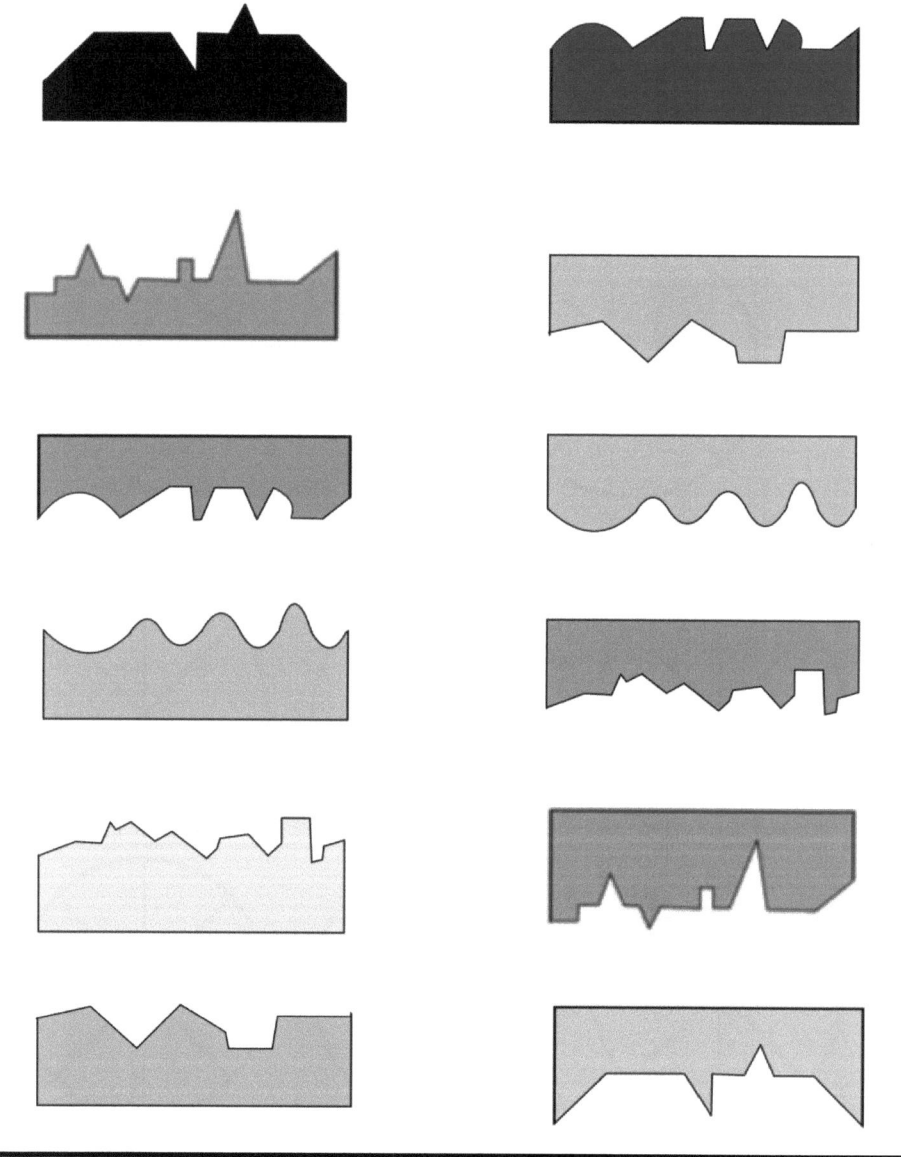

Here you see shadow images of animals. But the respective shadow image has divided into individual pieces of the puzzle. Which pieces belong to the respective animal? Connect them with a line!

If you look through a keyhole, you can't see everything. What animals/objects do you see? Write the number of the keyhole in the box on the next page!

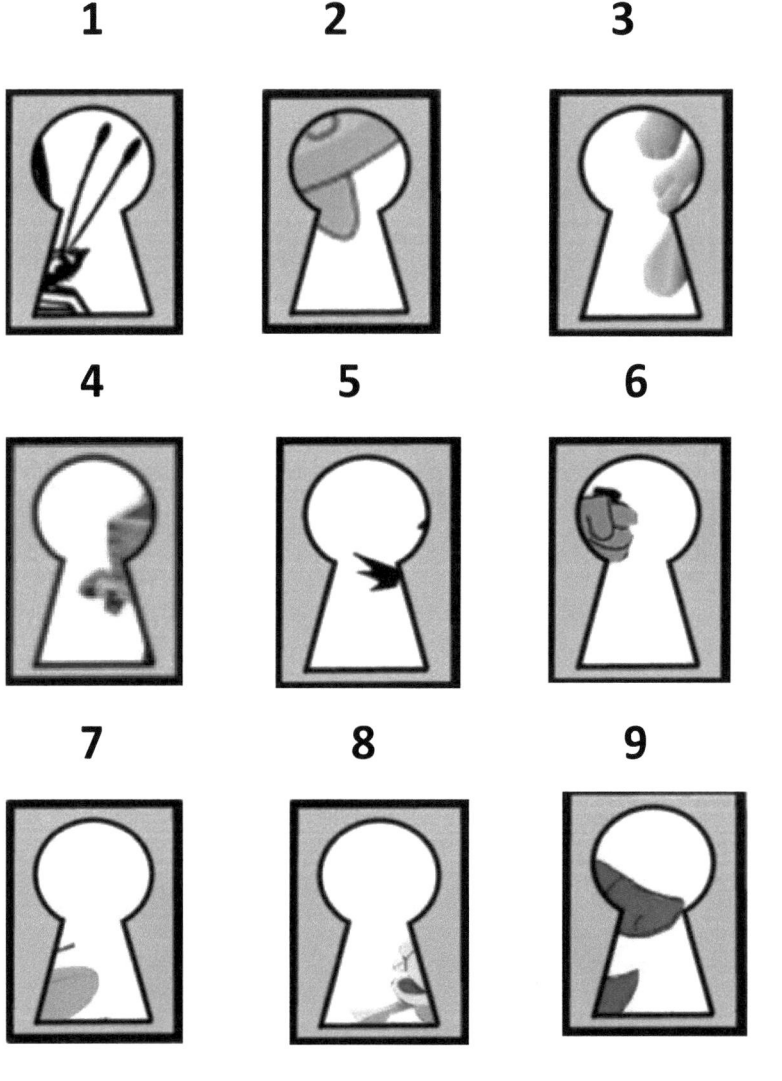

1   2   3

4   5   6

7   8   9

Domino/Sudoku

I like to play dominoes. The first 4 stones
I have already placed correctly.
Now I don't know how to go on.
Can you help me? I still have three
stones. Fill in the open stones with
the correct dots!

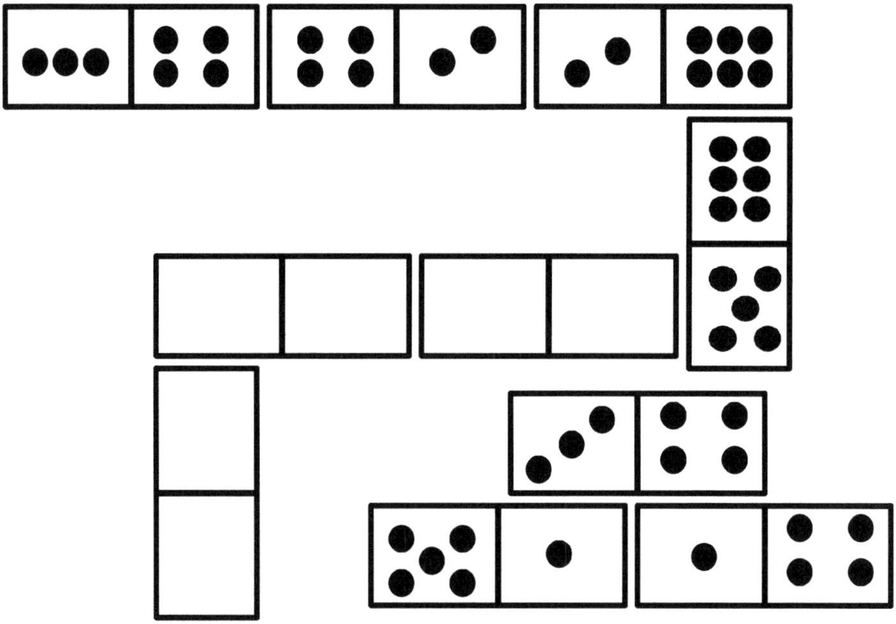

Fill in the empty stones with the correct
dots!

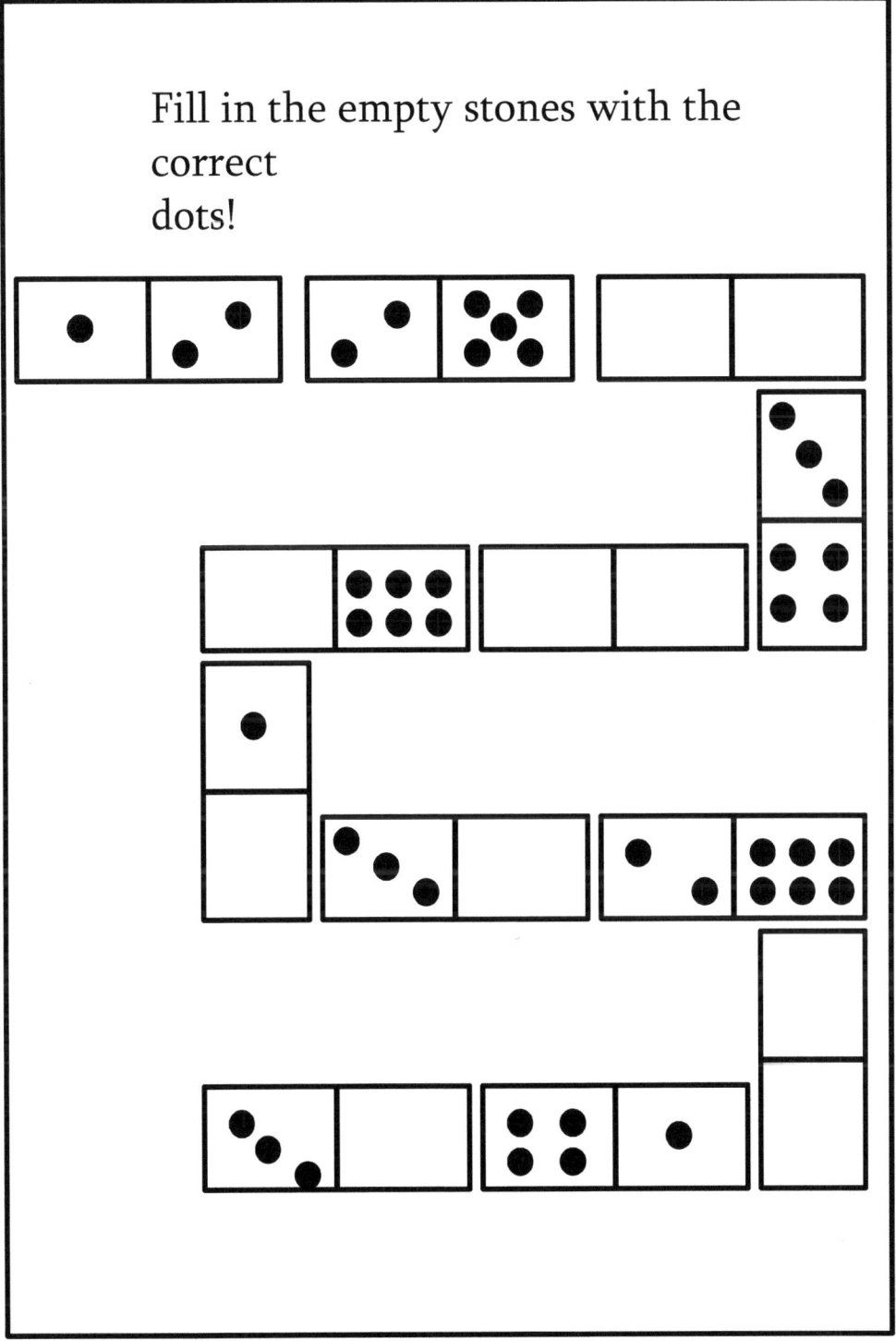

SUDOKU is a number puzzle. We take the number range 1 to 4 (1-2-3-4).

The empty squares are to be filled in such a way that in each horizontal row and each vertical column of the entire quadrilateral and within all numbers from 1 to 4 occur only once.

Here is an example:

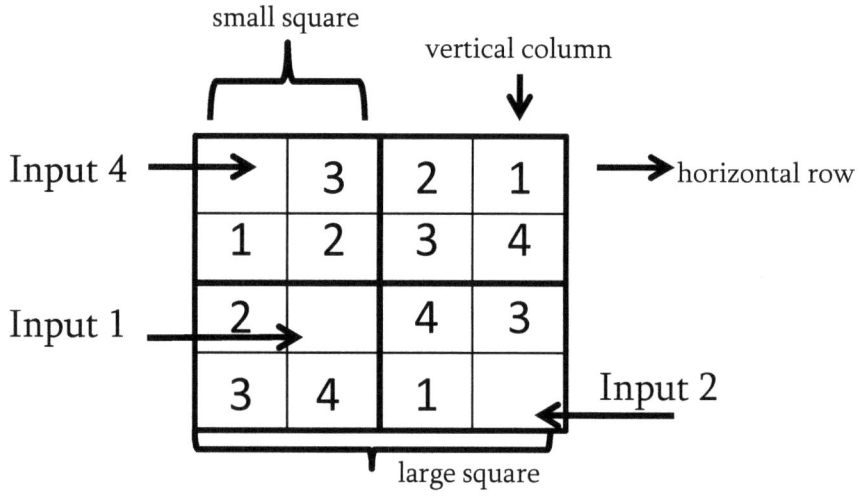

Try it! Every beginning is hard, but it gets better and better.

1		3	
4	3		1
	4	1	2
			3

2		4	3
3			
			4
4	2		

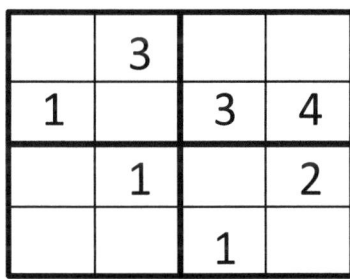

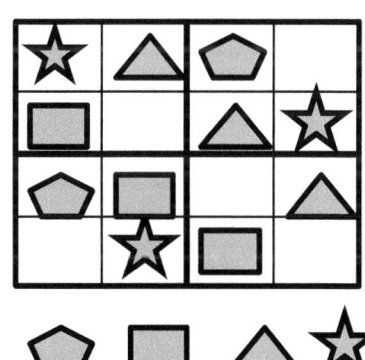

		2	1
1	2	3	
2		4	3
3		1	

4	3	1	
		3	
3	4		1
	1	4	3

	3		
1		3	4
	1		
3		1	

3		4	
	2		
		2	
	3	1	

2		4	3
3			
4	2		1

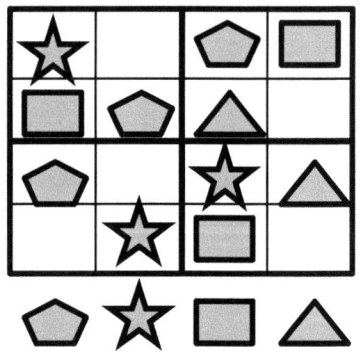

Numbers and letters

Connect the respective card to the correct one Group!

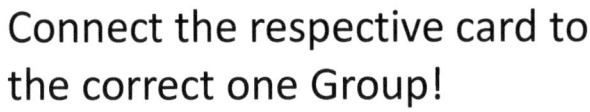

1	2	3	4	5	6
♥	♥♥	♥♥♥	♥♥ ♥♥	♥♥ ♥♥♥	♥♥♥ ♥♥♥

Connect the respective cube with the correct group!

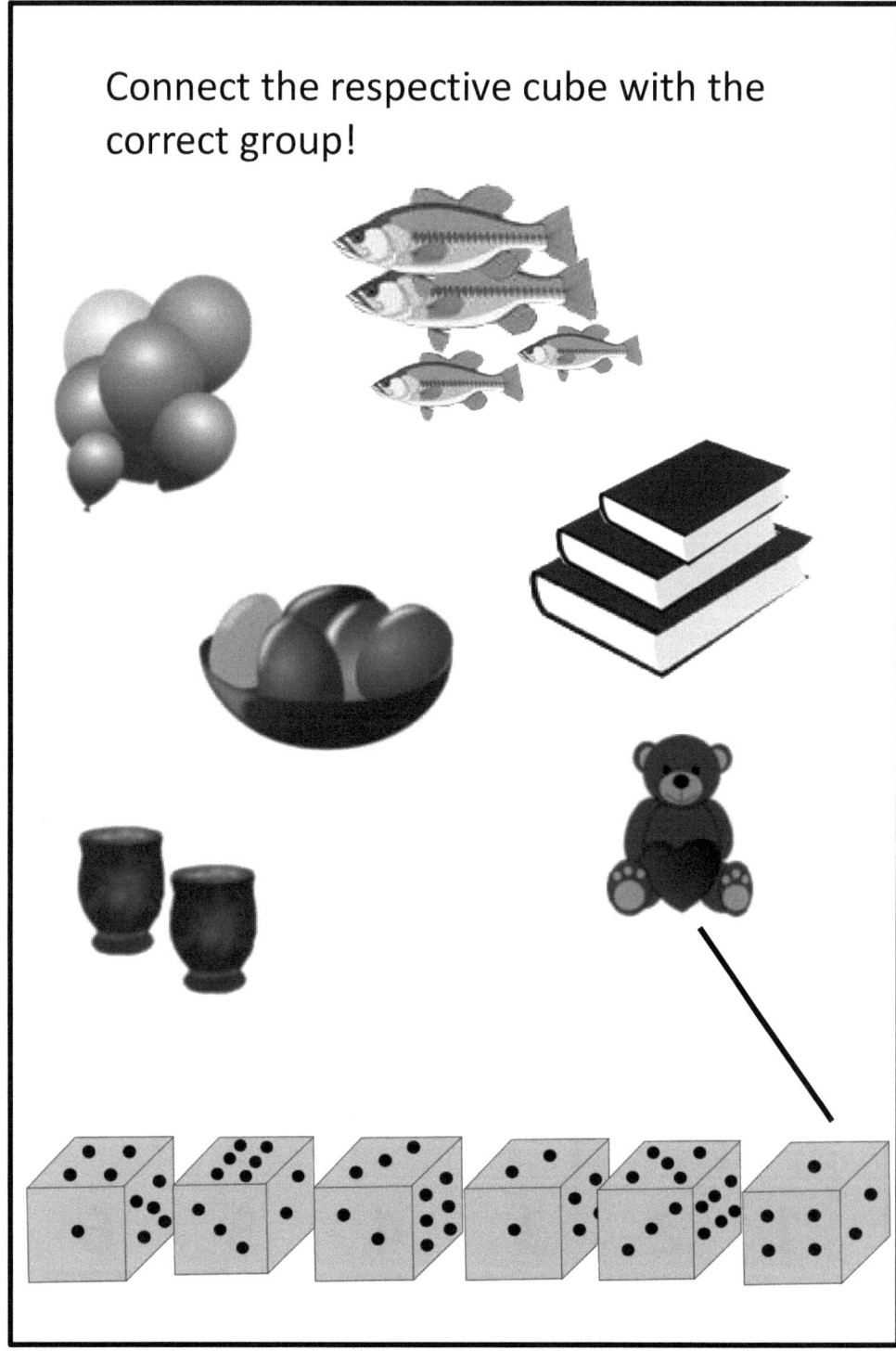

You did a great job. The series of numbers from 1 to 6 works very well already. Do you want to count to 10?

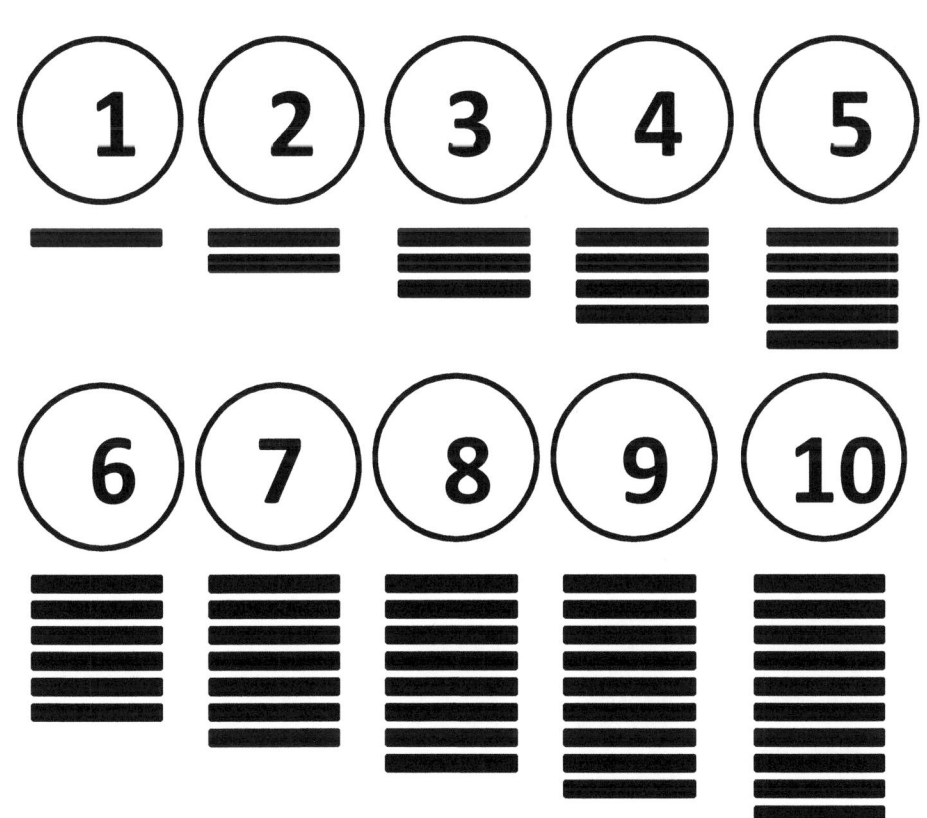

Oh dear, black bars have been forgotten in this picture.
Complete them with a pencil and count how many sticks there were. Write the number in the circle!

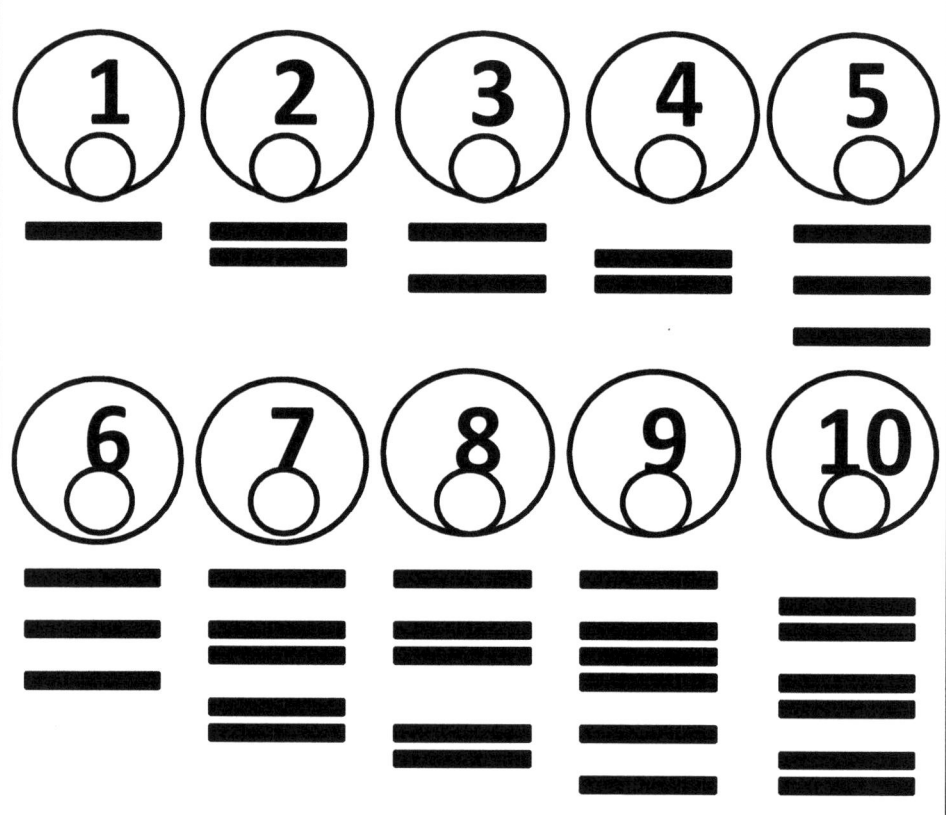

What number is behind the
question mark?

Solution: **1**

2	1
?	2

$2 + 1 = 3$

$? + 2 = 3$

↓   ↓

$2 + ? = 3$ $1 + 2 = 3$

3	1
?	3

? =

?	2
2	3

? =

4	?
2	4

? =

5	1
?	5

? =

"Anne, how many toys do you have?"

"More than you!"

Is that right?
Count our toys and write the result in the circle!
Who has more?

Look at the animals and say their names out loud.
Three animals start with a "B".
Mark them in the box with a pencil!

B

My name is Paule and my name begins with a "P". Look at the animals/objects and say their names out loud. 4 also begin with "P".
Mark them with a in the box with a pencil!

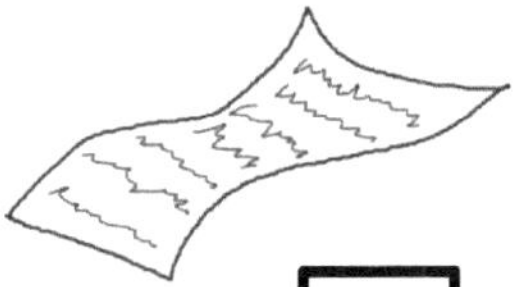

Dog breed

48

Look carefully at the pictures and say the names out loud. Say which letter the person/animal/object starts with.
The first letter is next to the picture.

Look carefully at the pictures and say the names out loud. Say which letter the person/animal/object starts with.
The first letter is next to the picture.

M

N

O

P

Q

R

S

T

U

V

W

X „X"

Y

Z

Yeti

Search picture and labyrinth

6 Changes

Search image 2: On the right-hand image some changes have crept in.
Find the difference!

How does the hare get to
the carrot?

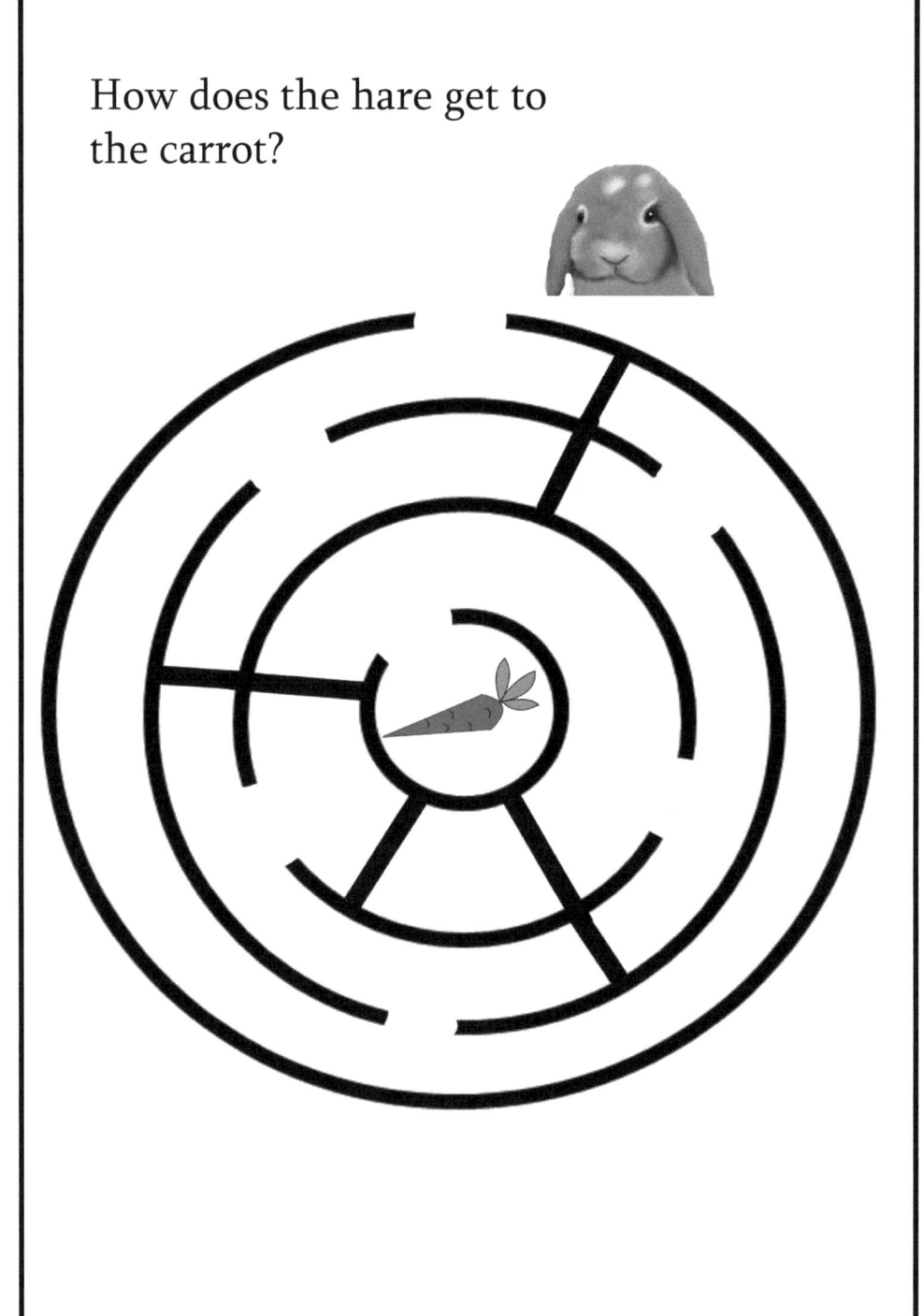

I want to visit Paule. Show
me the way!

How does the bird get its
food? Show him the way!

How does the monkey get the banana? Show him the way!

How does the bear get to the honey pot? Show him the way!

I am walking home. On the way I see many numbers.
Draw my path and count how many times I see the number "5".
Write the result in the box!

On the way to kindergarten I see many letters. Draw my path and count how often I see the letter "A".
Write the result in the box!

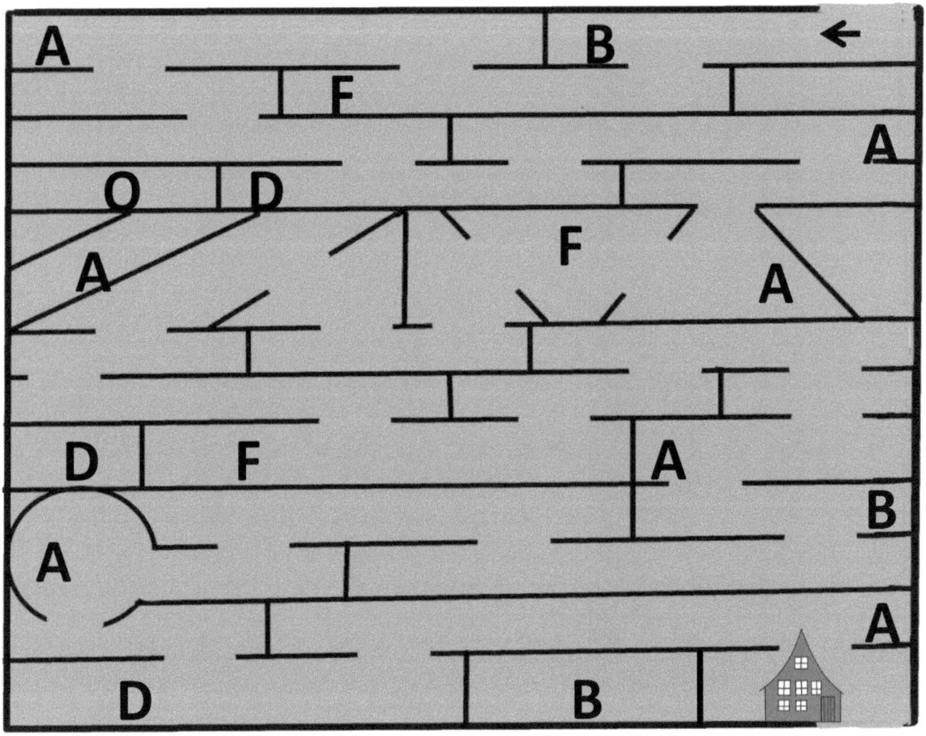

A B ←
F
A
O D
F
A A
D F A
B
A A
D B

Solutions

Page 5

Fish come out of the tap.
Correct answer: **no**

The rooster does not hatch the eggs.
Correct answer: **no**

Yes, the chicks are the children of the hen.
Correct answer: **yes**

Moles do not eat carrots.
Correct answer: **no**

Bees don't bite, they sting.
Correct answer: **no**

Locusts can jump one metre.
Correct answer: **yes**

Paule rides without a bicycle helmet. The lamp and bell are missing.
Correct answer: **no**

The boy has only 6 nuts, the girl has 7 sweets.
Correct answer: **no**

Absolutely not! Do not enter frozen lakes/ponds!
Do not enter! Danger to life!
Correct answer: **no**

A duck cannot hatch from a chicken egg.
Correct answer: **no**

Correct answer: **yes**

Page 11

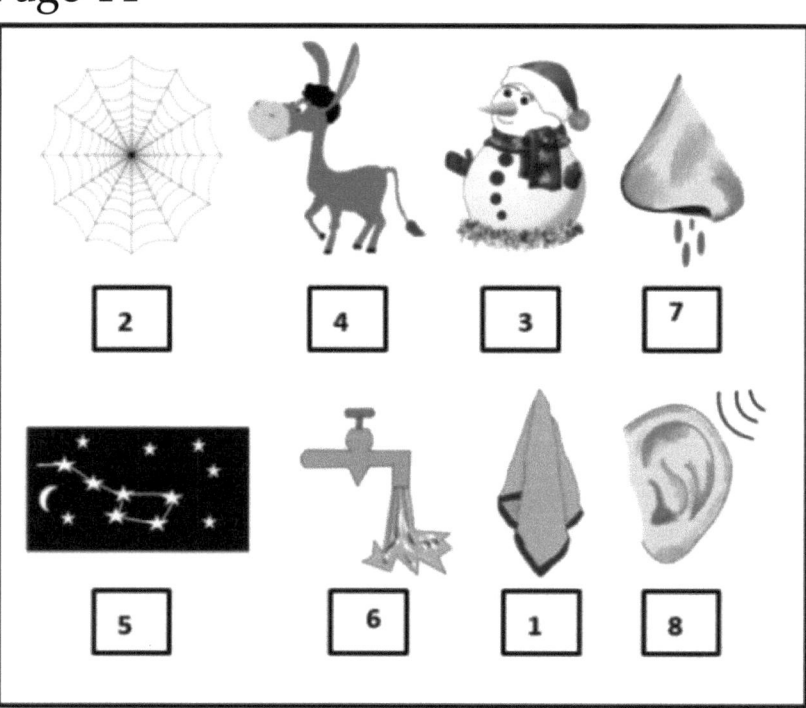

Page 18

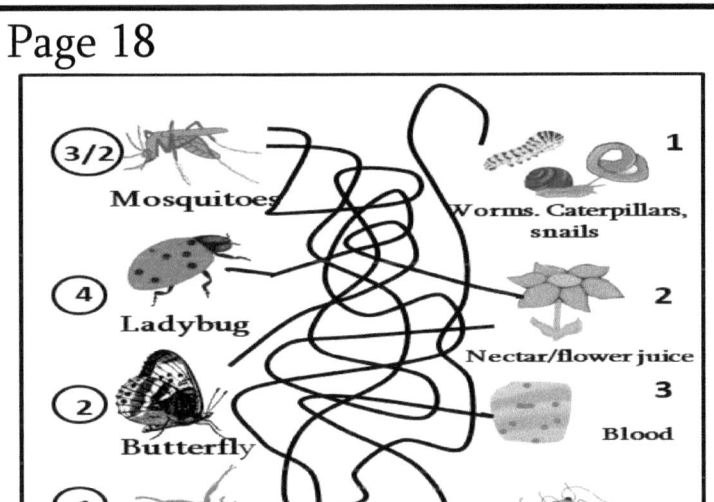

(3/2) Mosquitoes		Worms. Caterpillars, snails	1
(4) Ladybug		Nectar/flower juice	2
(2) Butterfly		Blood	3
(1) Beetle		Aphids	4

Page 21

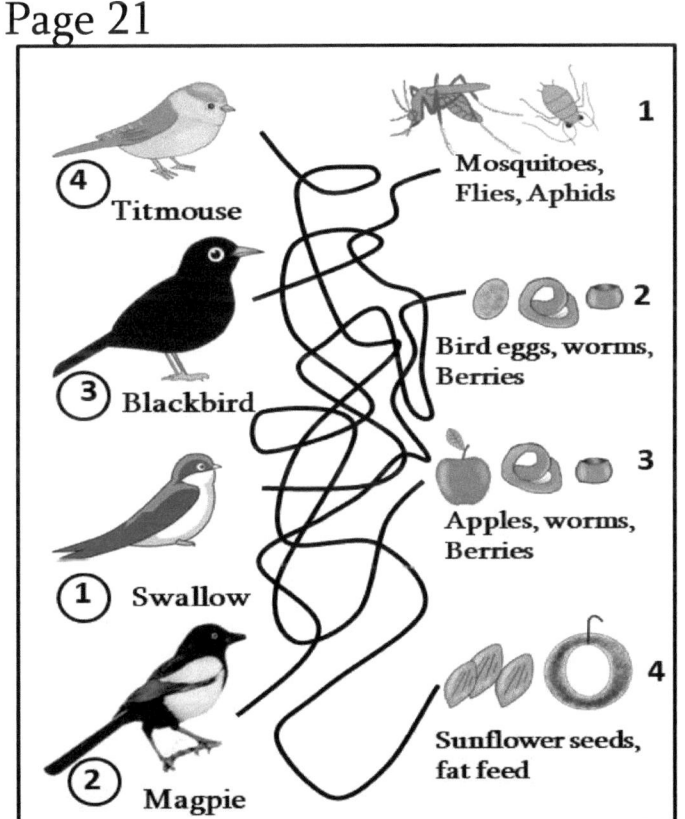

(4) Titmouse		Mosquitoes, Flies, Aphids	1
(3) Blackbird		Bird eggs, worms, Berries	2
(1) Swallow		Apples, worms, Berries	3
(2) Magpie		Sunflower seeds, fat feed	4

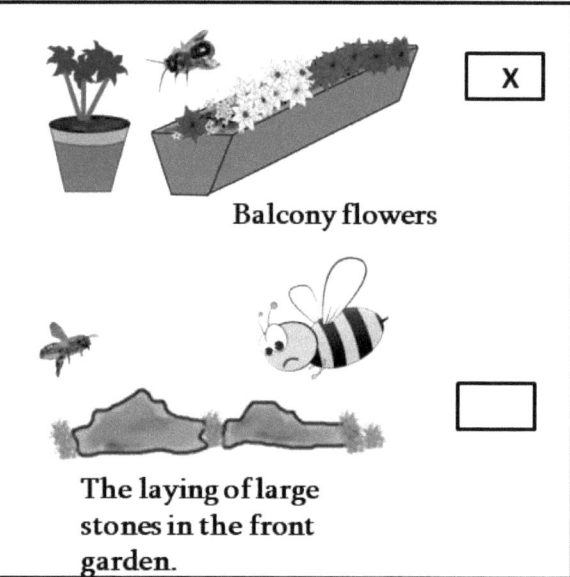

Balcony flowers

The laying of large stones in the front garden.

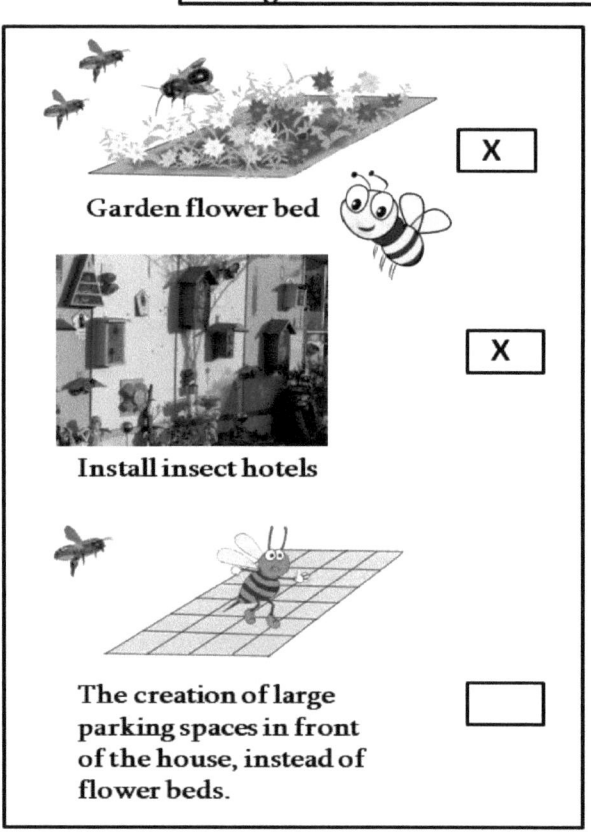

Garden flower bed

Install insect hotels

The creation of large parking spaces in front of the house, instead of flower beds.

Page 22

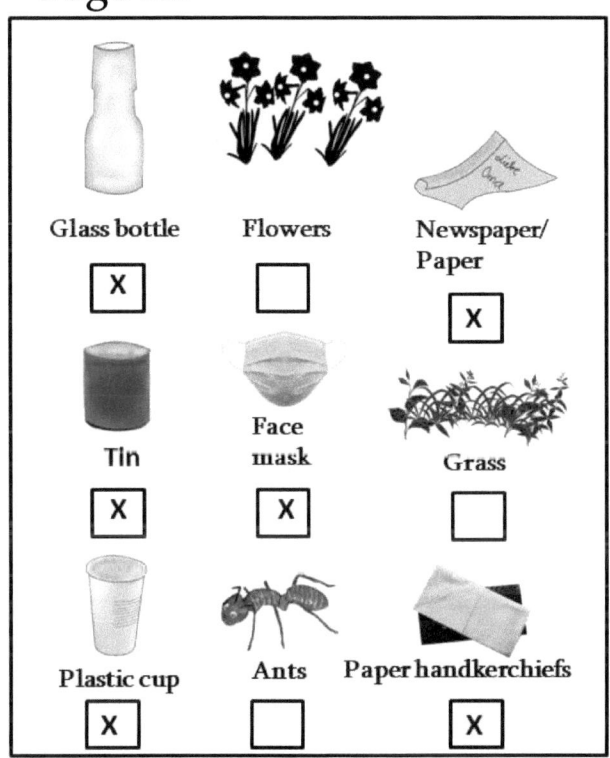

Glass bottle [X]	Flowers [ ]	Newspaper/ Paper [X]
Tin [X]	Face mask [X]	Grass [ ]
Plastic cup [X]	Ants [ ]	Paper handkerchiefs [X]

Page 23

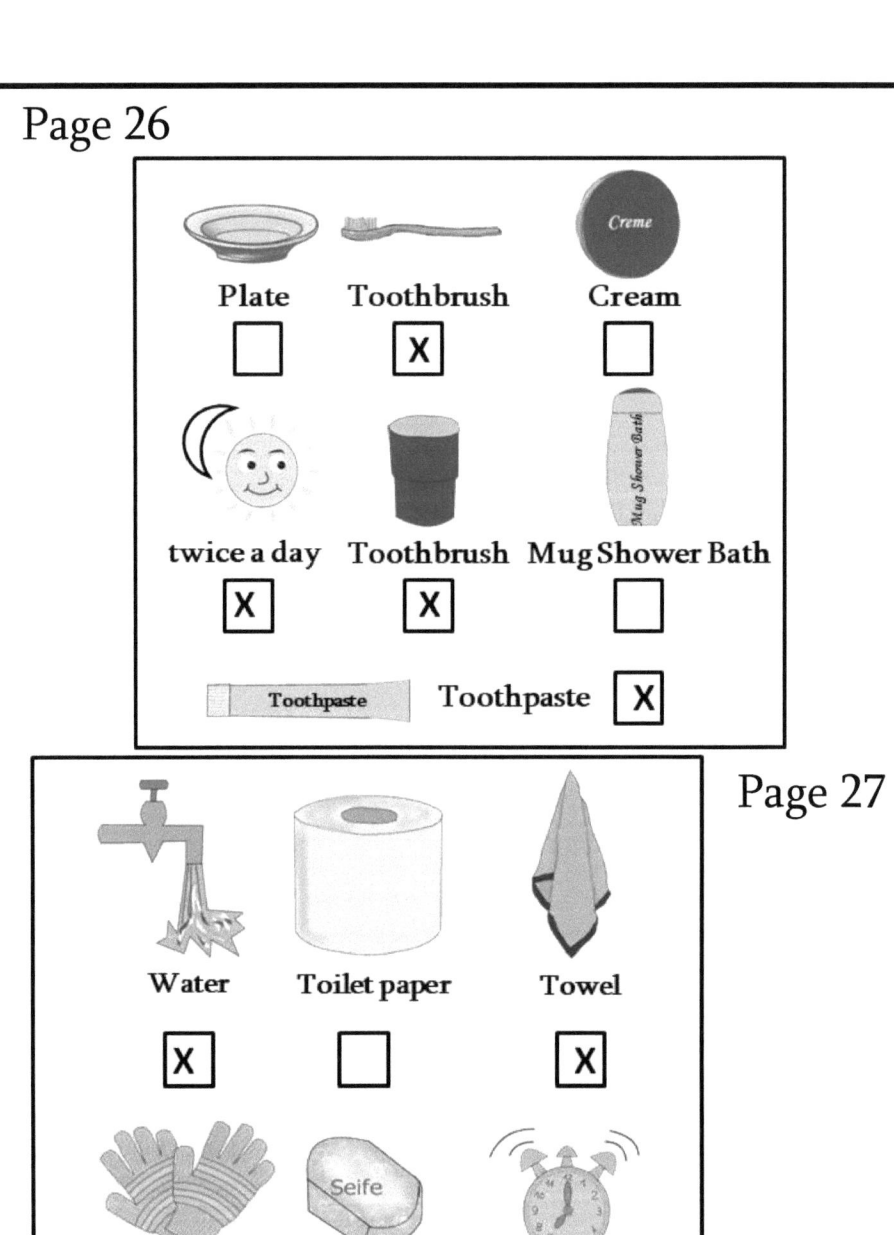

after the toilet

before the meal

X

X

after the evening
greeting on television

after feeding and
Petting animals

X

after the child
comes home

before playing
on the
playground

X

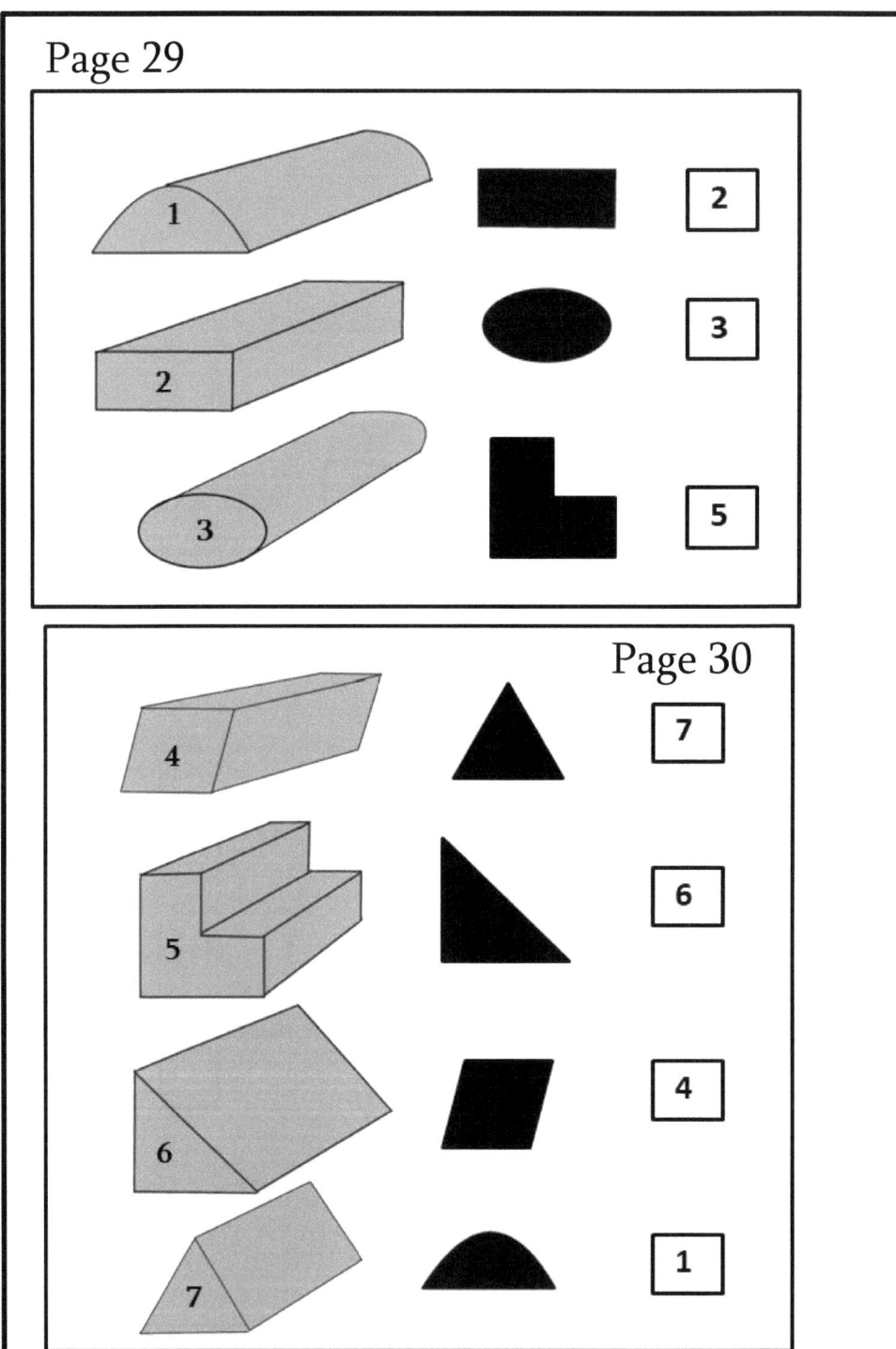

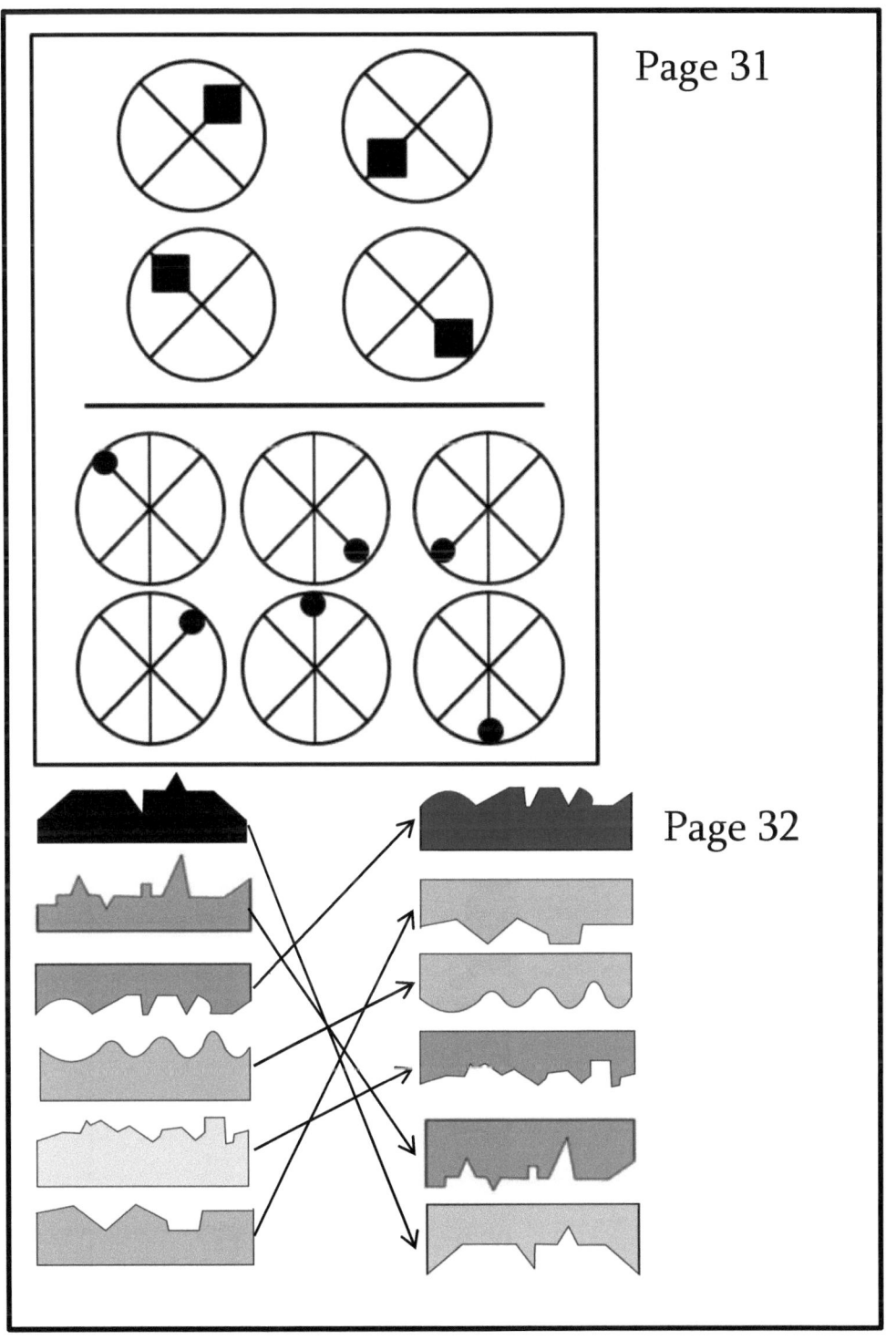

Page 31

Page 32

Page 33

Page 35

8	4	6
1	5	9
2	3	7

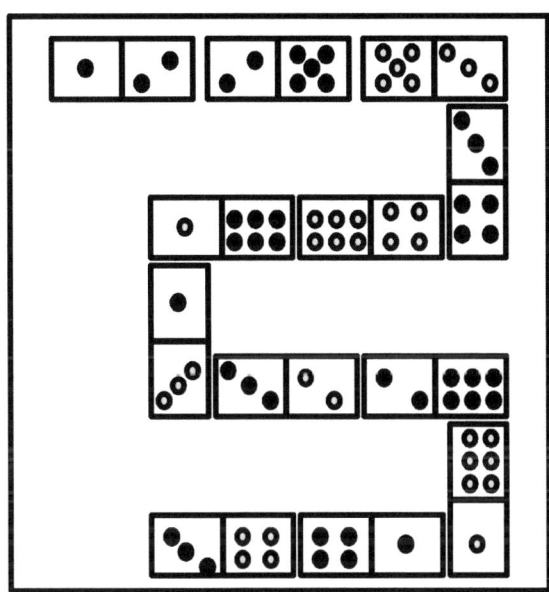

Page 39

1	2	3	4
4	3	2	1
3	4	1	2
2	1	4	3

2	1	4	3
3	4	1	2
1	3	2	4
4	2	3	1

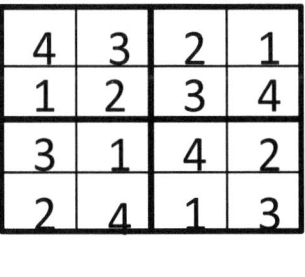

4	3	2	1
1	2	3	4
3	1	4	2
2	4	1	3

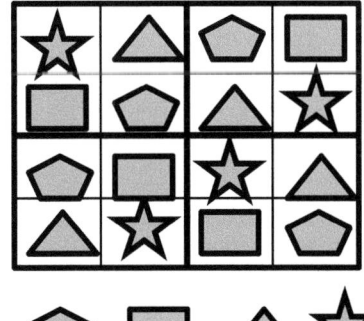

4	3	2	1
1	2	3	4
2	1	4	3
3	4	1	2

4	3	1	2
1	2	3	4
3	4	2	1
2	1	4	3

4	3	2	1
1	2	3	4
2	1	4	3
3	4	1	2

3	1	4	2
4	2	3	1
1	4	2	3
2	3	1	4

2	1	4	3
3	4	1	2
1	3	2	4
4	2	3	1

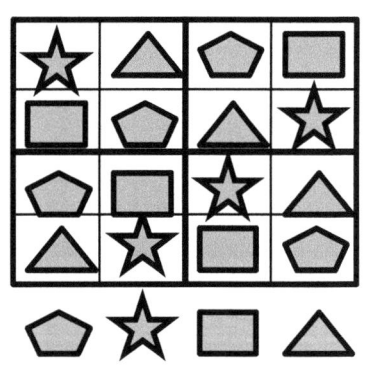

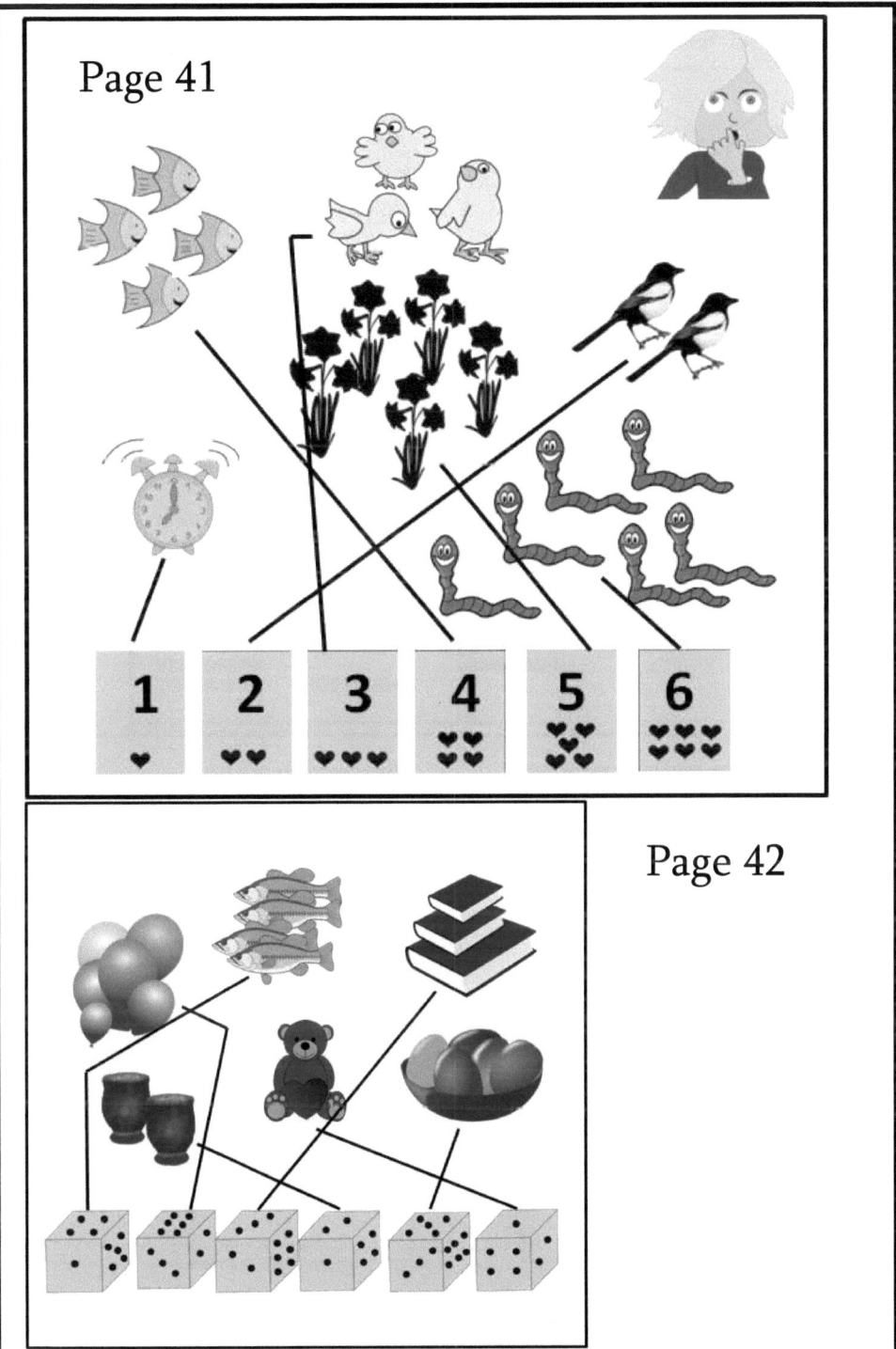

Page 41

Page 42

71

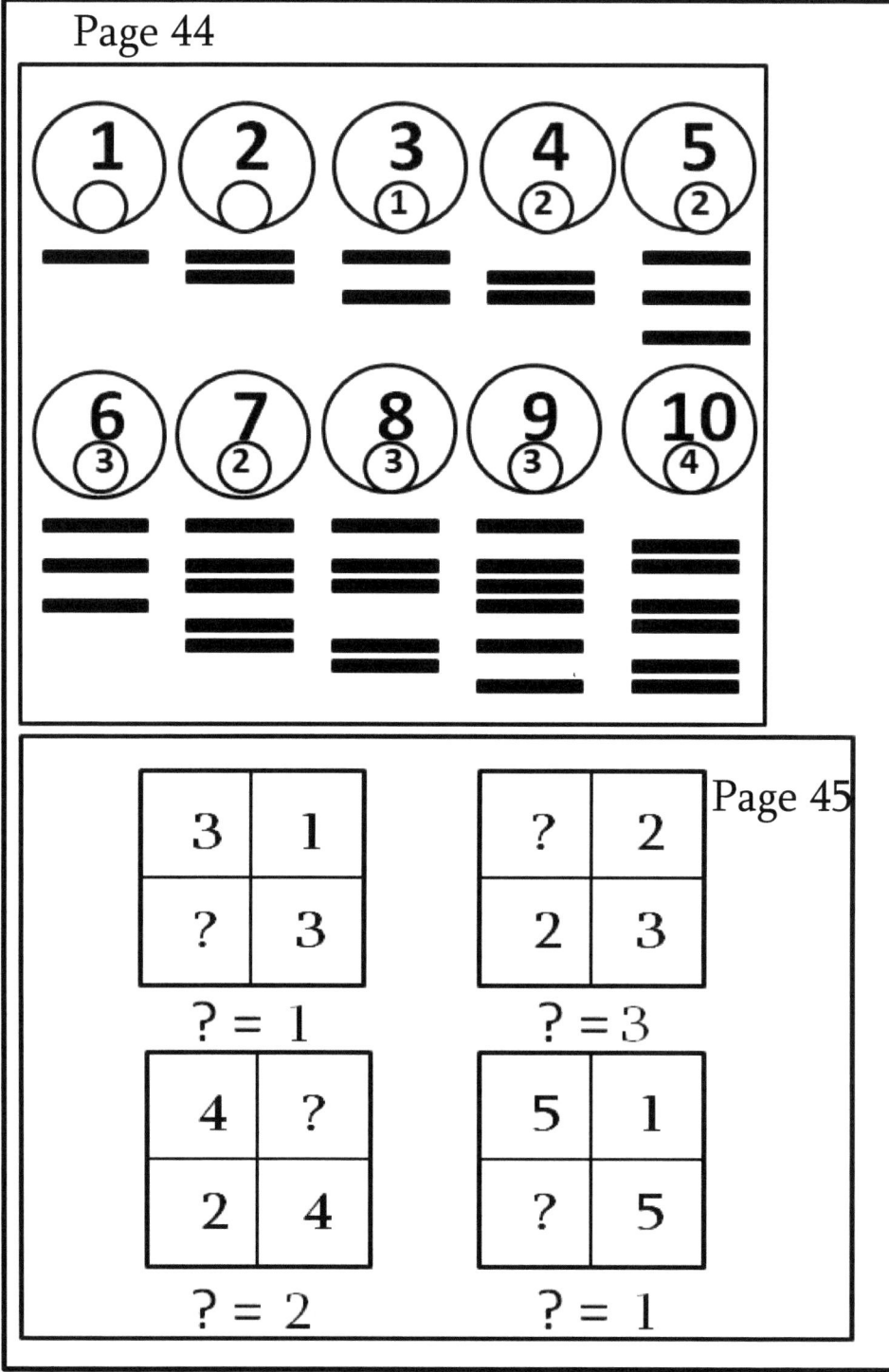

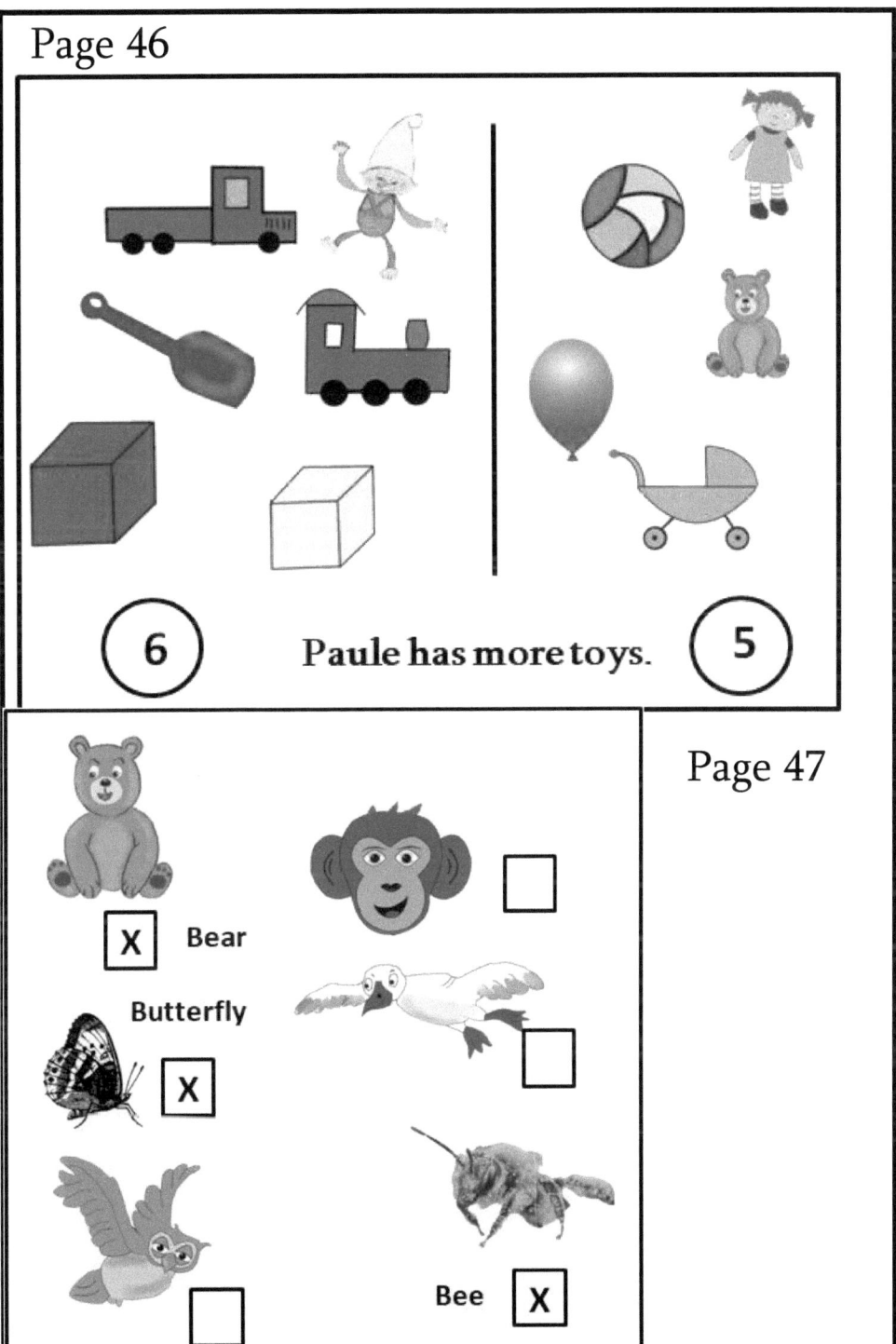

Paule has more toys. 6 5

Bear [X]

Butterfly

[X]

Bee [X]

Page 48

Paper
X
X
Poodle
X
Parrot
Penguin
X

Page 51

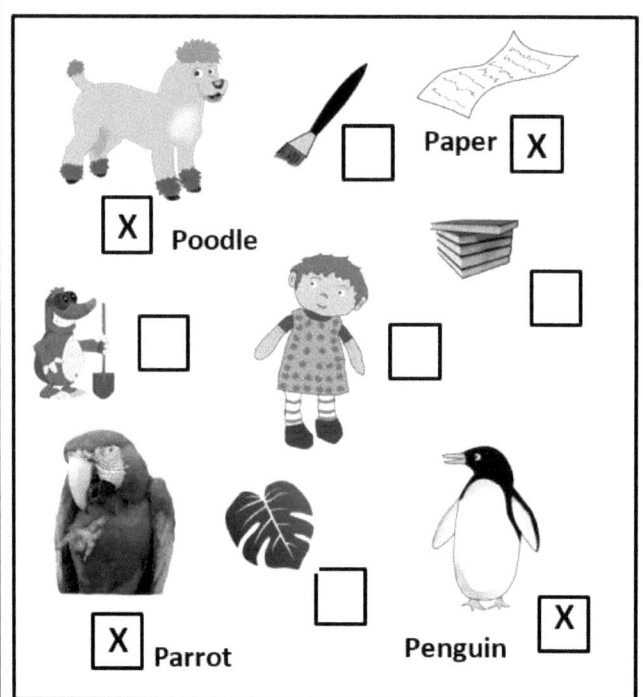

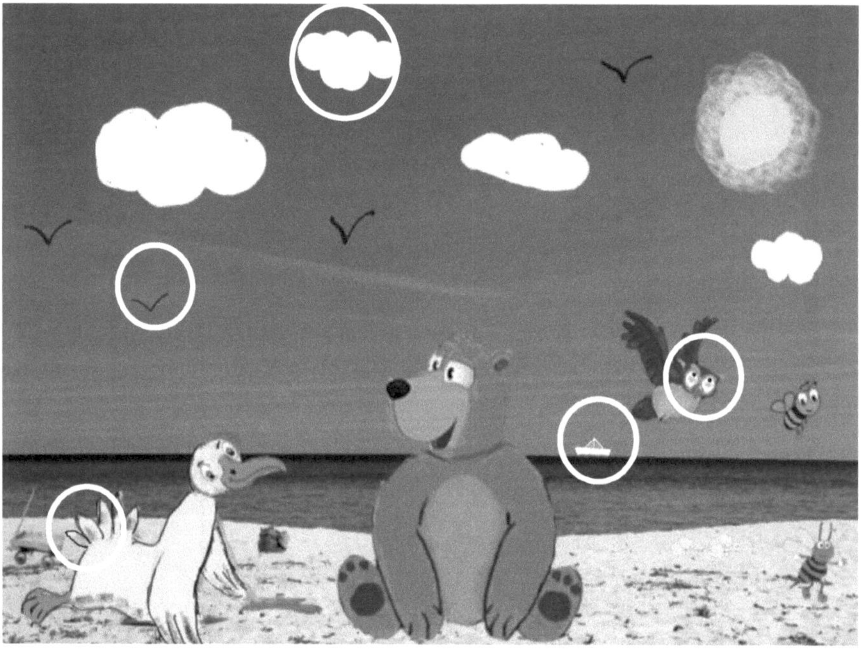

Page 53

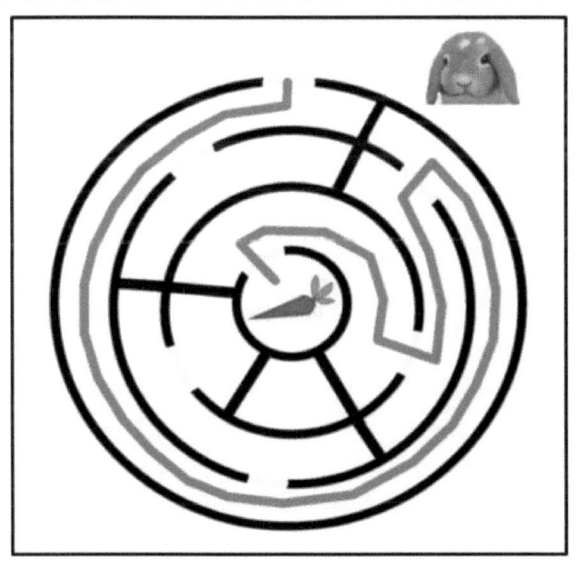

Page 54

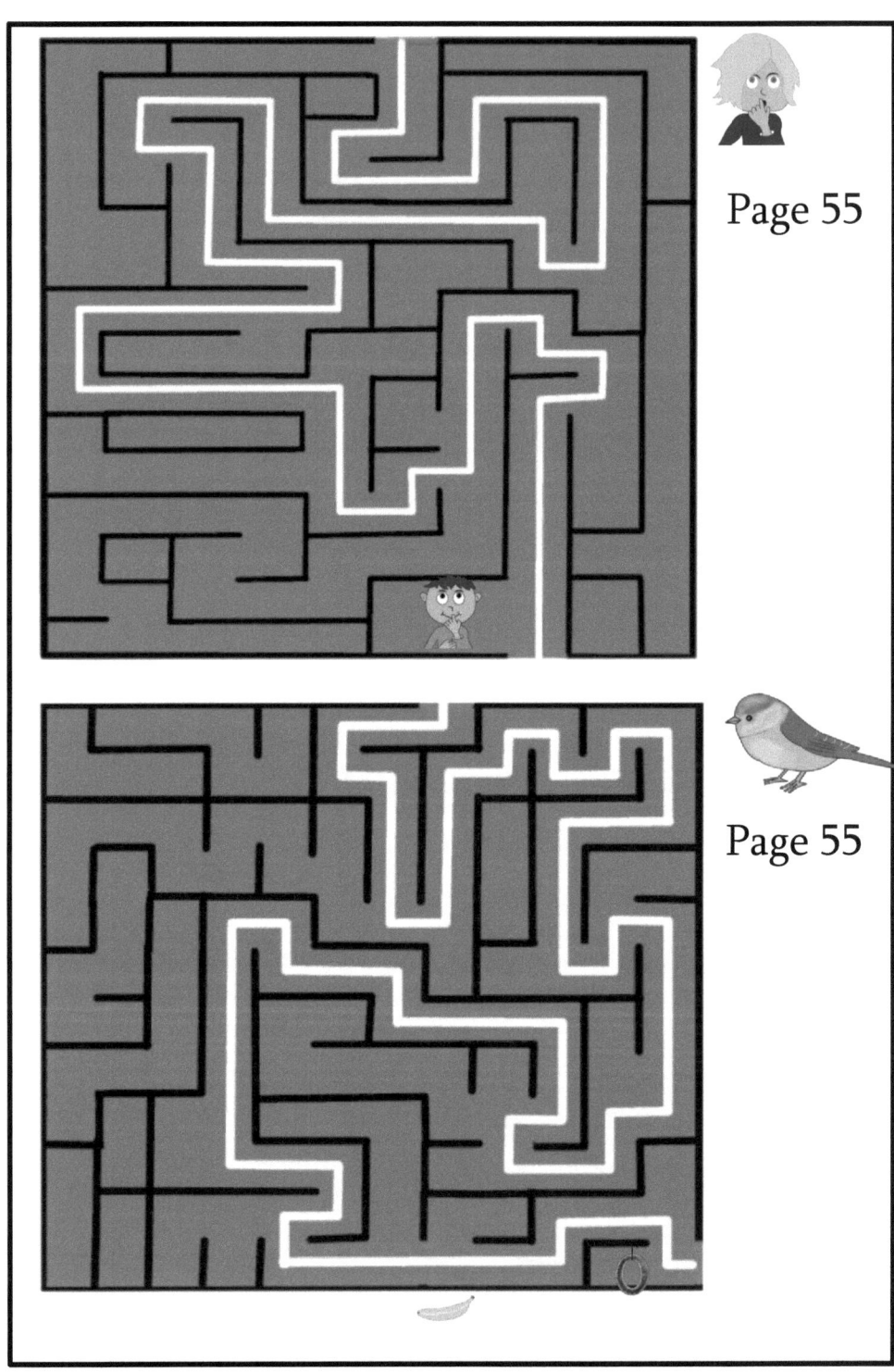

Page 55

Page 55

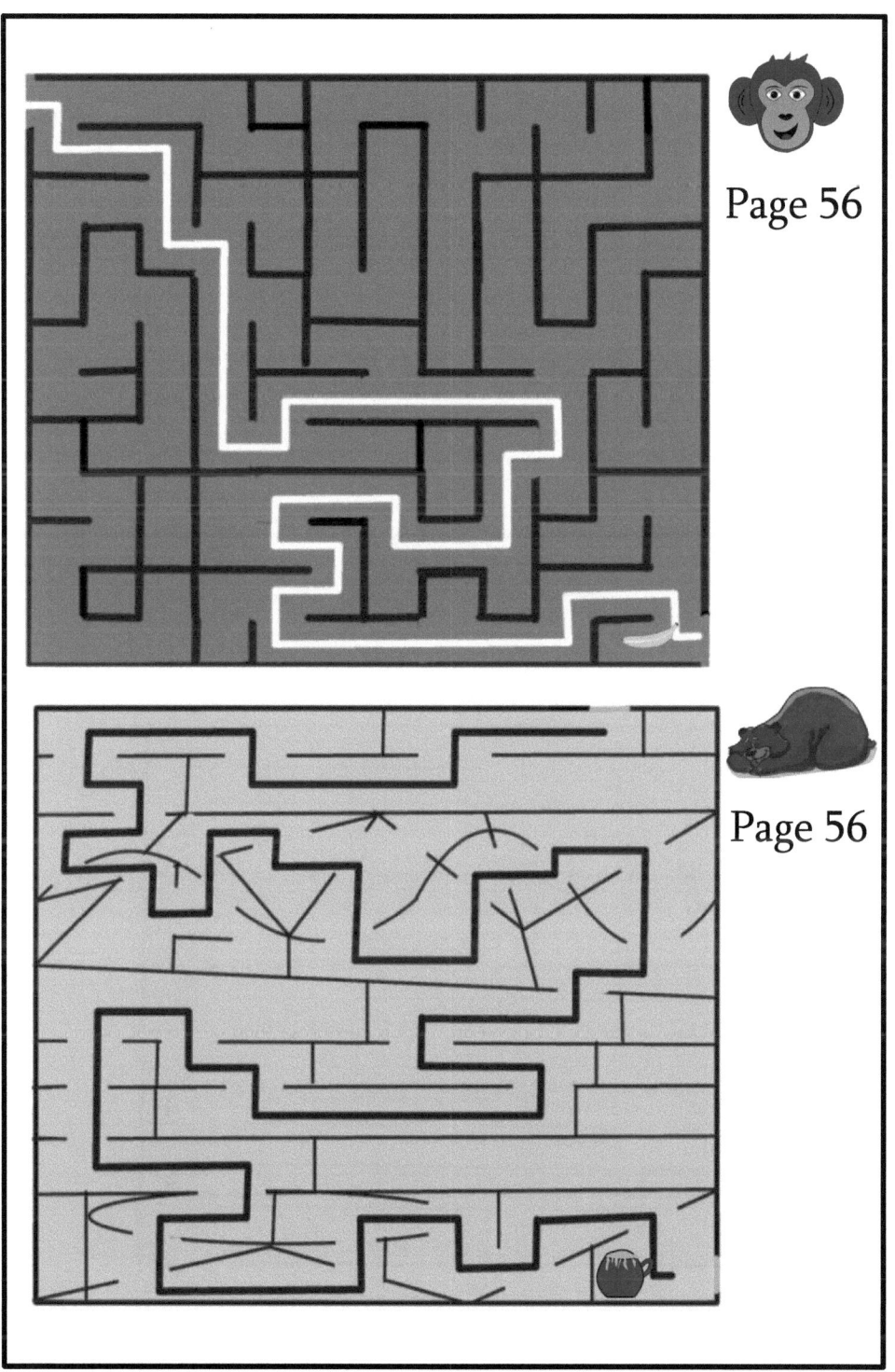

Page 56

Page 56

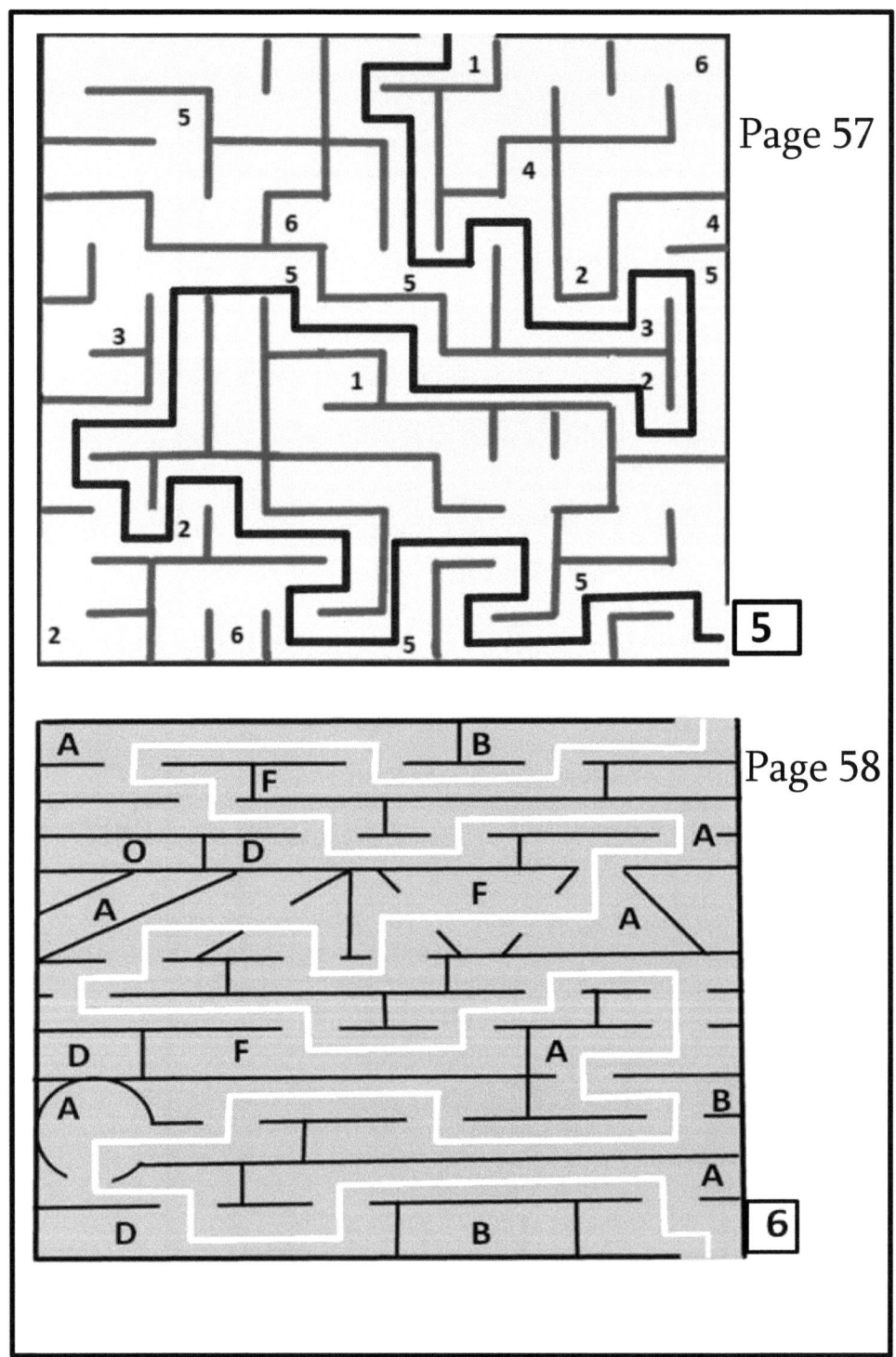

Page 57

Page 58

Hurray, you did it!
How did you like the puzzle book?
We would be very happy to receive a rating.
You can also contact us at the following email address, write to:
wolfgang-kulla@gmx.de
You are guaranteed to get an answer. We wish you all love and good! Keep being curious.
Your Anne and your Paule